EVERY
IDEA
IS A
GOOD
IDEA

EVERY IDEA IS A GOOD IDEA

❖

BE CREATIVE ANYTIME, ANYWHERE

How Songwriters and
Other Working Artists Get It Done

TOM STURGES

JEREMY P. TARCHER/PENGUIN
a member of Penguin Group (USA)
New York

JEREMY P. TARCHER/PENGUIN
Published by the Penguin Group
Penguin Group (USA) LLC
375 Hudson Street
New York, New York 10014

USA • Canada • UK • Ireland • Australia
New Zealand • India • South Africa • China

penguin.com
A Penguin Random House Company

Most Tarcher/Penguin books are available at special quantity discounts for bulk
purchase for sales promotions, premiums, fund-raising, and educational needs.
Special books or book excerpts also can be created to fit specific needs.
For details, write: Special.Markets@us.penguingroup.com.

Library of Congress Cataloging-in-Publication Data

Sturges, Tom.
Every idea is a good idea : be creative anytime, anywhere   /   Tom Sturges.
p.   cm.
ISBN 978-0-399-16603-7
1. Creative ability.   2. Creation (Literary, artistic, etc.).   3. Creative thinking.   I. Title.
BF408.S836   2014   2014016117
153.3'5—dc23

Printed in the United States of America
1 3 5 7 9 10 8 6 4 2

BOOK DESIGN BY TANYA MAIBORODA

CONTENTS

FOREWORD

ALMOST EVERY TEENAGER I MEET WANTS TO be a rock star, or perhaps a writer of hit songs, and they imagine it is a cakewalk. It certainly is not.

All the creative people that I know have to work hard to achieve their goals. Okay, everyone has a good idea from time to time, but do they follow it through?

It needs inventiveness and hard work, and this book is an extraordinary examination of the whole process of creativity, something within the capability of everyone.

—Sir George Martin

PREFACE

T O DISSECT, STUDY, TEACH, AND ANALYZE the creative process takes enormous insight and balls. I personally was thrust into the creative process by accident and luck. Having just become head of Columbia Records—straight from being the chief lawyer for the company—I had no idea I could be "creative," no idea I could have "ears," no idea that the world of music could unleash a passion of creativity that exhilarates me to this day. And when, in interviews, I'm asked how I discovered the artists I've signed or the songs I've chosen for artists to record, I usually shrug my shoulders and say it was a natural, undiscovered, unknown "gift." But was it?

Well, after reading this very enlightening book by Tom Sturges, he challenges that notion for me; but more important, challenges that notion for what I hope is a vast multitude out there who want to explore whether they are creative or whether they can be creative. And he does it with color, with recalled experiences, with candor, with entertaining stories and anecdotes that entrance and fascinate the reader. I know that after reading this book there will be countless revelations and confessions from those who were stimulated and motivated to look deeply within and alter the course of their career or their life.

—*Clive Davis*

INTRODUCTION

I HAVE BEEN PART OF THE MUSIC BUSINESS FOR more than twenty-five years, most of that time as a music publisher. I was executive vice president and head of Creative for Universal Music Publishing Group. I was president of Chrysalis Music Publishing Group. I was a song plugger and talent scout for Screen Gems–EMI Music Publishing, and started as a professional manager for Arista Music Publishing.

I can recognize talent in others and I can hear a hit song. I see what writers and artists are going to *become* as much as see who they are sitting in front of me, with the only evidence that matters being their songwriting ability. More than two hundred writers signed music publishing deals to companies I worked for, and many of them achieved lasting worldwide success. Among these were Billy Corgan of Smashing Pumpkins, Outkast and Goodie Mob, 50 Cent and G-Unit, 3 Doors Down, both Antonina Armato and Tim James of Rock Mafia, Slaughter, Green Jelly, Chris Brown, and Jack Johnson. I also signed Foo Fighters and Blink-182; writer/producers Troy Taylor, Mark Batson, and Jason Epperson (aka Jay E); and rapper and champion basketball player Shaquille O'Neal. I acquired rights for several writer/artists who had only one defining hit in their careers, including Baby Bash ("Suga Suga"), Vanessa Carlton ("A Thousand Miles"), Afroman ("Because I Got High"), Montell Jordan ("This Is How We Do It"), Katrina and the Waves ("Walking on Sunshine"), and Owl City ("Fireflies").

I was also a song plugger and placed more than eighty songs. A song plugger finds a song its home by pitching it to the right artist for a recording. I gave Huey Lewis and the News their breakout single "Heart and Soul," and Pat Benatar her worldwide hit "We Belong." Aretha Franklin and George Michael got "I Knew You Were Waiting (for Me)" and won a

Grammy for it, while Celine Dion took "Think Twice" to the top of the UK charts and won an Ivor Novello Award for Song of the Year for writers Andy Hill and Pete Sinfield. I suggested Mariah Carey record "I Still Believe" for her *Greatest Hits* album. She had sung backup on the original recording with Brenda K. Starr many years before, so maybe that was a no-brainer. In total, the writers I signed have sold more than 175 million albums, over 26 million singles, and more than 18 million downloads, written fourteen #1 singles, and won twelve Grammy Awards. So far. There is still more to come.

At various times I was also point person for Jon Bon Jovi and Richie Sambora, Prince, Carole King, Billy Idol, Beastie Boys, Sinead O'Connor, Jethro Tull, and U2, but had nothing to do with their discovery or signing.

Being surrounded by all this talent gave me a rare opportunity to learn about the creative process, because I was right there. As it happened, I watched, I listened, and I learned. I took notes and asked questions. Anytime any of the writers or artists who have graced my life began to start on something, I paid attention. I never knew I would write a book about it, but I found myself in a place of such trust and closeness within their lives that I could not help but inhale.

I have observed creative genius unfettered and unfolding in its natural habitat . . . over and over and over again, for years. How many people can say that?

Does that make me an expert in creativity? Is there even such a thing? I would rather be considered a patient observer of the art, a collector of its techniques, its likelihood and promise, someone who has grown familiar with creativity's nuances and possibilities.

And here's what I've come to believe. Creativity is a gift, from life to us. It exists in varying degrees, measures, and amounts in each of us, but we all have it inside. There is as much creativity in our lives as we allow there to be. On this point, Maya Angelou said you can't use up creativity because "the more you use, the more you have." Creativity is a reliable source of our self-respect, innovative power, and intellectual achievement. Tapping into this force—whether to paint an oil painting, write music, design a home, shape an advertising campaign, or discover the cure for cancer—this is when we are most human. Coincidentally, this is also when we are at our most vulnerable, most likely because the tenderness of our new ideas makes us so. While not everyone can paint or sculpt, write a symphony, or imagine a building, creativity can become a greater part of any life, enriching and ennobling it in many different ways.

The physical process of creativity, regardless of the field or area in which it is used, is the same process. Regardless of the creative challenge we might be faced with, our brains respond the same way, they do the same thing. Neurons signal one another over synapses, often millions at a time, and spray one another with a substance that serves as an activating mist. This happens no matter what the new thoughts are, or what the subjects of those thoughts are. The spray, most often glutamate, serotonin, dopamine, or acetylcholine, is like an idea lubricant, and we all get plenty to work with. If you are a chef nuancing a recipe or a fashion designer working on a little black dress, you are utilizing the same brain functions and having the same aha moment as a film composer writing a score or a songwriter finding the perfect chorus. *The brain cannot tell the difference.* It is a machine functioning as designed. And if that's all there is to it, why not have more creativity in our lives?

❖

Over the past fourteen years I have introduced more than a thousand public school students in the Los Angeles area to the basics of creativity, as a test of my own belief that creativity can be taught and learned, like English or math, and that it can be practiced and developed, like basketball or golf. I teach them that creativity is a skill.

Some of the students are in Gifted and Talented Education (GATE) programs, while many others are at-risk inner-city students. Some come from amazing circumstances, but many do not. I had an idea that the more creativity these students had in their lives, the better those lives might be, and every class proves it again and again. I introduce the students to the breadth of their creative instinct and provide them with techniques that they can utilize to access it at any time, as much as they want or need to, for the rest of their lives.

The students learn the basics of good creative thinking by learning how great thinkers—including several songwriters and composers—often think. They learn how those people guided and nurtured their own passions and intellects, whether challenged or inspired to do so. The students learn how to expand their own intellectual capacity by understanding how the greatest music makers, such as Mozart and Beethoven, developed and searched their own intellects for ideas and possibilities. By the end of the class, most of the time students are able to see and practically touch their own creative spirit by becoming engaged in the challenges and exercises put before them as part of the process of "learning" creativity.

The classrooms are my laboratory. Teaching the students how to create is the experiment. The songs and lyrics and stories they write are the product. Watching them discover their own instinctive creative humanity, in bursts and flashes of creative thought and outright passion, is joyous proof of the hypothesis that creativity *can* be taught and learned. For those students who were already creative and in touch with their intellectual instincts, the ability to more readily access those instincts was significantly enhanced.

Seeing this process repeat over and over, for many years, revealed to me the possibility and even the likelihood that *anyone and everyone* can learn to be more creative—not only students, or younger people, but everyone.

⟡

In the pages that follow, many examples, ideas, guidelines, and exercises will be presented to you. Once you begin to understand how some of the greatest creators who have ever lived created, you will begin to better understand how *you* can create. You will recognize and direct your own creative thought processes better by learning how these geniuses did it when faced with the same dilemmas. With their experiences as your model, you will better understand how to imagine and encourage your own ideas, and how to think, understand, and harness the best of your own creative power. If everything goes according to script, the methods you discover will be available to you whenever and wherever you need them, for the rest of your life.

Imagine being able to understand and manage your own creative process, manipulate its power and capability, and maximize its output, simply because you have the tools to do so. Imagine being able to encourage and harvest your own daydreams and musings, simply because you have found a way to filter out the least valuable ideas and focus only on the gems. Imagine being able to give your mind a creative assignment and have the patience to wait for it to arrive, the result of a clear understanding of the capacity of your own intellect when left to its own devices.

Only a small percentage of people will ever develop the ability to render rooms speechless with their paintings or sculptures or improvised storytelling. Only the tiniest subgroup of people will redefine fashion and couture. Fewer still will write lyrics or melodies to hit songs. But creativity comes in many forms and formulas, not just poetic or artistic gifts. Top-level marketing and advertising companies are very creative places, as are architecture firms. The best trial lawyers and schoolteachers and chefs are highly creative. All of these areas of expertise require constantly innovating thinking if lasting success is to be achieved.

This book is meant to be a toolbox full of possibilities, any one or ten of which might provide you with the guidance and inspiration you need to break through to and engage your creativity more fully. If you can become a more creative thinker, you will be a better problem solver because your mind will give you more options to consider. You will be a better decision maker because you will be able to imagine the future more clearly, and you will be able to better predict the likely results of your choices. You will be a better creator because you will use significantly more of your intellectual capability than you knew how to set free before.

Creativity is the most individual and unique gift you possess. It is what allows you the freedom to be you. But the magic of creativity is different for everyone. So, too, is the journey of creation. The joy of realizing that you can repeat that moment again and again, whenever you need it, will be unspeakably beautiful. With the right tools in the right hands, it is not only possible to achieve greater creativity on a regular and repeatable basis, anywhere and anytime; it is impossible *not* to achieve it.

As you read on, and new ideas occur to you, write them down, treasure and preserve them, and save them for some future creative project. Let none of them just slip away. Fill in the margins of these pages with your notes and reactions and, hopefully, inspirations. If that does not give you enough room in which to capture your musings, consider a devoted notebook or computer file that fills up as you go along. Summarize in your own words an essay or passage, if it strikes you like that. Try the exercises—they all really do work. Grow more and more aware of the process of your own creativity, the bursts of light and possibility as they take place, the tingle that accompanies new thoughts. Become knowledgeable about when and how you create best, where your new ideas sneak up on you most easily. Mozart wrote that ideas filled his head when he went out for a walk. Where will your creativity find access to you?

Almost every technique to enable creativity that I have ever seen or heard about is somewhere in this book. The same is true for every trick of the trade that I observed about creators. Songwriters are just the starting point—I have sought knowledge and wisdom about creativity from many sources. This brought me to look at the brain, discover who the very first creators were, and then investigate the creative magic of a television writers' room as a way to better understand group creativity. I also went looking for examples of what Picasso and Michelangelo knew about their creative powers, in addition to what Carole King, Paul Simon, and Marilyn Bergman know about theirs. The processes and methods these creators have *already* discovered could be the ones you are still looking for.

It has brought me incredible joy to witness the beauty of creativity so many times, in so many different people, under so many different circumstances. My hope is that I successfully convey this to you, and give you a better understanding of how creativity can open a thousand doors in your life, any one of which is your future.

But to hear it knocking, you must know what it is.

CREATIVITY:
AN OVERVIEW

WHAT IS CREATIVITY?

Many people think of creativity as some glamorous, elegant practice that only certain people get to do, but this is not really so accurate. For Michelangelo, creativity was grabbing a hammer and a chisel and banging on a piece of iron-hard marble for months and months, as he had to do in order to create just one of his masterworks, the *David*. Creativity was also him building a system of scaffold platforms that stuck out from holes in walls, hundreds of feet in the air, which allowed him to stand and paint with his arms above his head *every day for five years* to finish the ceiling of the Sistine Chapel. He endured paint and dust getting into his eyes, and an angry, impatient pope complaining that he was taking too long to get the job completed. There was nothing glamorous about it.

Or take multiple-award-winning songwriter Diane Warren, who you will meet soon, who goes into a cramped and tiny office on Sunset Boulevard every single morning at 8:30. With plaster raining down from leaky windows, and used lyric sheets and old song ideas gathering in growing piles, she sits there alone and creates. Her superstitions will not allow her to upgrade to more luxurious accommodations. Always on her own, just her, her intellect, an old keyboard, and a drum machine. No red carpet, no adoring fans, no glamour. No matter what happened or didn't happen the night before, every single morning she is there, creating.

Creativity is actually many things, and it encompasses many definitions. According to Noah Webster and his dictionary, it is "artistic or intellectual inventiveness." David Kelley, founder of Stanford University's Institute of Design (known as the d.school), said in an interview, "Creative confidence is like literacy." Albert Einstein was quoted saying, "Imagination is more important than knowledge." Antoine de Saint-Exupéry, author of *The Little Prince*, wrote about creativity in that wonderful book: "A rock pile ceases to be a rock pile the moment a single man contemplates it, bearing within him the image of a cathedral."

Thinking is an involuntary act, believes Dr. Mark Jude Tramo. He is a neurology and ethnomusicology professor at the Herb Alpert School of Music at UCLA, and the director of the Institute for Music & Brain Science. He provided many insights and details about the brain for this book, as you will read later on. According to him, creativity is simply part of our basic makeup, encoded in our DNA, and a key advantage of our genetic endowment. It is inherent in our wiring as human beings to look at the world and see that it could be something different: to visualize a home where there is just a plot of land, or a nation where there are just a few disagreeing states, or a city where there is just a gas station and some sand. All of these were, at some point, brand-new ideas. Every "thing" started out as just an idea to someone. Our imagination and its simple wanderings are our creativity at its most basic. It is our nature to imagine, and to imagine that more can be done with what we have been given. "It is the fulfillment of our most basic human instinct to be creative," says Tramo.

Nobel Prize–winning neurophysiologist, scientist, and brain researcher Dr. Torsten Wiesel discovered how the brain processes light images by identifying ocular dominance columns in laboratory animals. He and his partner, David Hubel, shared the prize in 1981 for discovering how visual information is transmitted and processed in the visual cortex. This is a man who spent his life and lifetime's work in a lab, but he recently wrote to me about creativity. He said, "In the arts and the sciences, a creative or inspired mind is always the driving force behind original and beautiful work."

In a much simpler forum than the ones Dr. Wiesel occupies, I recently posed the question "What is creativity?" to a group of at-risk inner-city public school students I was mentoring in South Los Angeles. There were about thirty of them. They were invested and intrigued, willing to learn and willing to participate. Way in the back, a young man named Nestor put his hand up and answered the question with one of the most accurate definitions I have yet heard. He provided the room with the magic and purpose of the individual creative intellect in one little sentence. He said, "Creativity is what makes you *you*, different from everyone else." It stopped me in my tracks. It was so exactly right. When I asked him if he had just thought of that, he said that yes, he had. So in addition to being brilliant and insightful, it was a brand-new idea. And that's what makes it perfectly creative.

To me, creativity is any idea that has never been thought before. It is both the flash of a single idea or the long dawning of a group of ideas that might have taken months to emerge. As you will read, many creators let their ideas steep in the stew of their intellects for weeks, months, or sometimes even years. But creativity is also the nuanced development of an existing idea, like a better mousetrap or a new iPhone app, or the careful enhancement of a concept already in use, as you see in style and couture every year. It can also be inventing an entirely new and remarkable concept, like the telephone or the camera or the iPod or the theory of relativity. Creativity is a force that happens anywhere, anytime, and often uncontrollably. Whether artistic, mechanical, musical, athletic, poetic, explanatory, illustrative, scientific, or strategic, creativity is what makes you *you*.

A PATH TO SELF-RESPECT

A woman named Allee Willis is the co-writer of many hit songs, including Earth, Wind and Fire's "September" and "Boogie Wonderland"; "I'll Be There for You," the theme song to the television show *Friends*, which she cowrote with the Rembrandts; and many of the lyrics for the Broadway musical *The Color Purple*. Thanks to her great success, she now lives a life of complete creative freedom. She does little except think and dream and imagine and explode with new ideas every minute of every day.

We were walking around her big pink house one morning, talking about how she pursues her muse, how she lets her creativity take flight, and how she finds new inspirations every day. She said that she achieves this by letting absolutely nothing get in the way of a creative thought. She leaves the business to others in her life, for instance, and hasn't tried to balance her checkbook ever. That's right, ever. I was telling her how I use creativity as a key element of my volunteerism with public schoolchildren and she responded by saying this: "It's a very good thing that you're doing. *The path to self-respect goes through creativity.*"

I had never heard a statement so true and so alive with purpose. I adopted it immediately, made it my own, quote it endlessly, and frankly, try to live by it. Her words guide my interactions with songwriters, artists, executives, students, mentees, practically everyone and anyone. The path to self-respect *does* go through creativity. The more we create, the better we feel about ourselves. The better we feel, the more we feel like creating. The more we feel like creating, the more we get out of it. The more we get out of it, the better those ideas are. The better the ideas are, the more we respect ourselves for having them. And so on. It's an endless cycle of good, a never-ending circle of growing self-respect.

The young people who know me only as a volunteer think I am teaching them creativity and how to better write, draw, paint, and design. But really I am teaching them to respect themselves, stay in school, graduate, live great lives, eclipse their circumstances, and make a difference in the world, no matter the humble beginnings. At a certain point, they cannot help but begin to think more graciously about themselves because they have grown to completely respect their own creative capabilities. They begin to like themselves more readily, to believe in themselves more passionately. They begin to live in a world where creativity is a foundation to a greater and ever-growing sense of self-respect.

THE CREATIVITY DISTRICT— AN IMAGINING

New York City has Wall Street and the Financial District, Palo Alto has Silicon Valley, and I imagine that our brains must have a Creativity District. It's down one of the millions of dark avenues inside there, somewhere near the cerebral cortex. In it there are hundreds of clusters of thousand-story buildings, all bunched and crowded together.

On every floor of every building, different ideas are being developed and manufactured, all of them at variously different stages of production. There is a constant hum, and the air reeks of excitatory spray. The elevators in these many buildings—and there are millions of them—can move up, down, sideways, laterally, circularly, or elliptically in an instant, stopping on any floor for any reason whatsoever. The elevators can also zip into and around any other creativity building just as easily as one would hope, and all the energy from one building can be borrowed by any project in any other building. It is a totally communistic environment, making a network of powerful, high-energy thought factories. Working together they have perfected systems to invent, reinvent, write and rewrite, imagine and reimagine, all day every day, no matter what. The output is limited only by the amount of input—the district will create whatever it is asked to create.

The Creativity District inside us, working in, on, and around all those thousand-story buildings, can accommodate and contemplate any number of ideas, and devote whole floors to work on them, if necessary, for as long or as little an amount of time as needed. The precious attention of our conscious minds may be busy with a crossword puzzle or another session of Angry Birds, but that does not mean we cannot ask our intellect to come up with solutions to our problems, write papers, solve economic conundrums, or give fresh consideration to old song lyrics. The brain has never been ruined by having too much to do and, in fact, may actually thrive on having too much to do.

Part of learning to be creative is learning to accept that our minds can exist on several floors of several buildings at the same time, working through a hundred ideas at the same time, as it is doing right now while you read this page. You plod through these words, and meanwhile your intellectual mind is whipping around all over the place, writing a book or a screenplay, thinking about how to advance your career, wondering what to say in the big meeting tomorrow, still trying to understand what love is, or what to cook for dinner, or considering a big trade in the stock market, and possibly hundreds of other tasks.

As you will read shortly, some of the most successful creative people in the world simply give their intellect an "assignment" to create, and then go on about their busy lives. They are able to multitask far better than the rest of us because they have learned the joy of trusting in what happens in all those buildings down there in the Creativity District.

SOMETIMES CREATIVITY IS BORROWING

Novelists, storytellers, filmmakers, inventors, and patent holders—all are notorious borrowers. Nobody is really creating anything all that new anymore, not because they cannot come up with it, but because there is nothing to come up *with*. Aristotle, Mark

Twain, Charles Dickens, and Shakespeare came up with practically every possible story, and it's been nothing but borrowing in that field ever since.

As Mark Twain himself wrote, "There is no such thing as a new idea. It is impossible. We simply take a lot of old ideas and put them into a sort of mental kaleidoscope. We give them a turn and they make new and curious combinations. We keep on turning and making new combinations indefinitely; but they are the same old pieces of colored glass that have been in use through all the ages."

Upon his death, Picasso's principal studio in Mougins, France, was revealed to contain rooms within rooms, and, in the last room, one of his great secrets. It was a vault with a combination lock on the door, which, when opened, revealed an incredible treasure. In it were several original paintings by many of the world's great masters. Picasso was not only a creator of great art, he was a collector, too. Scattered around these masterworks were Picasso's studies of them, in which he openly copied precisely how Gauguin or Degas or Rembrandt might have brought a face to life, or manipulated a shadow in a garden, or captured the magic of a hand holding another hand. Not only would he study the genius of those who came before him, he would actually attempt to duplicate each stroke of the brush of the painting that moved him, that inspired him. He openly admitted this, remarking once about how he was quick to recognize and borrow the genius of those who preceded him. He even said, "Bad artists copy. Great artists steal. . . ."

At the time of Picasso's death, in order to pay his estate tax, the nation of France made a onetime exception and allowed his collection of paintings to suffice as payment of his taxes, in lieu of cash. The paintings were not auctioned or sold privately. After being evaluated, the works were distributed among museums all over the country. According to the attorney who worked on the transfer of Picasso's assets, this was the only time such an arrangement had ever been offered. It speaks to Picasso's genius not only as a creator but as someone who was able to recognize genius in others.

Does 100 percent of a new idea have to be new? Suppose only a small percentage of it actually is, and the rest borrows from here and there, with a collage of other people's ideas already mixed in. Standing tall on the shoulders of those who came before us is not only not illegal, sometimes it's called inspiration. Mozart listened well and borrowed heavily from the sound and art of Haydn, and part of his genius came from not being threatened by Haydn's greater experience and accomplishments.

During a lecture on the history of music at the Aspen Ideas Festival, Wynton Marsalis described the British Invasion of the 1960s' pop music scene as ". . . an echo of the blues, brought back to us without the black faces." And there is ample evidence that the Beatles, the Dave Clark Five, the Rolling Stones, Eric Burdon & the Animals, the Kinks, and many others listened fervently to America's rhythm and blues, or "race music," particularly to Bo Diddley, Chuck Berry, Willie Dixon, Little Richard, and Sam Cooke, and returned it to the American public. Also according to Marsalis, Muddy Waters said once about the Rolling Stones, "They stole my music but gave me a name. . . ."

Borrowing is an accepted part of the tradition of creativity, though within accepted guidelines. Renowned songwriter and Grammy Award–winning producer Simon Climie still recalls a warning he heard from an older songwriter when he was just starting out, who told him, "If you want to stay out of court, never steal *two* things from the same song."

Einstein was also very clear on this point. He said on a number of occasions, "Creativity is just knowing how to hide your sources."

CREATIVITY DOES NOT
REQUIRE EXPERTISE

One intriguing aspect of creativity is that one does not have to be an expert in a particular field in order to be a creator in that field. One does not have to possess greatness at a skill in order to be passionate for it and, within that passion, creative for that skill. Take the incredibly difficult and almost-impossible-to-master musical instrument the violin. You will read evidence later on that Beethoven could hardly play it, despite writing a significant portion of the symphonic canon for that instrument. He could "hear" in his mind what notes he wanted the instrument to make, though he could not make those sounds himself. Does that lessen the force of his writing or the significance of his impact on the world in any way? Not at all. He did not need to play the instrument to write for it.

The same holds true in other fields. Screenwriters rarely act the parts they write. Fashion designers almost never fit into the clothes they dream up. Songwriters have exercised as much license in this area as anyone: many of them can hardly put more than a few notes together when it comes to singing. But who really cares? All that matters is the end result when it comes to creating. The performance is a thing better left to performers. There is a musician and songwriter named Burt Bacharach. With Hal David he created some of the most iconic pop songs ever, including "Raindrops Keep Falling on My Head," "Promises Promises," and "Close to You," plus hundreds of others. When he performs, his voice is so rough that his own songs are barely recognizable when he sings them. Surrounded by background singers and a big band, of course you know them instantly. But the point is that he cannot sing anywhere near as well as the performers who brought and continue to bring his songs to life. Does it really matter? He created the songs, so who cares if he can sing them?

Suffice it to say, this metric is illustrated over and over in numerous fields and pursuits. Choreographers only have to dream it up; they don't have to dance it. Advertising companies do not expect their executives to produce and edit campaigns; they only need to come up with the ideas for them. And as is the case with many architects, Frank Lloyd Wright did not build his houses; he just thought of them.

Creativity does not necessarily require expertise. And the ability to perform perfectly what one has created is not central to being successfully creative.

CREATIVITY IS DISRUPTIVE

Business schools call it disruptive technology when someone figures out a way to do something newer (i.e., smarter or quicker or easier) than a previous iteration. The automobile was a disruptive technology to the buggy whip and horse businesses, just as much as Velcro wiped out the use of buttons and zippers in millions of products. Television was a cataclysmic earthquake in the landscape of early radio, until cable television grandly disrupted the entrenched world of antenna-based TV. And then the defining "new" of this generation, the Internet, has changed everything about the way we do everything.

In another day and age, a bridge builder named Gustave Eiffel won a creative competition to design a welcoming archway for the 1889 Paris World's Fair, celebrating the centenary of the French Revolution. In a café in Paris, in a puff of creative simplicity, he sketched the shape of his idea on the back of an envelope. It was almost entirely new and, as he envisioned it, it would result in the tallest structure in the world, dwarfing the skyscrapers of New York and the pyramids of Giza. His entry triumphed over all the other applicants' entries and his design immediately went under construction. Until the last rivet got welded and the whole thing didn't fall down in a giant heap, it was thought to be literally impossible to accomplish. Nothing like it had ever been constructed. Nothing like it had ever been *thought of* before. It was that new, and that much of a disruption. Using eighteen thousand pieces of pig iron, weighing in at seven thousand tons, Eiffel changed the way modern man looked at himself and what he could achieve. He showed the world that creativity had no limits. His great idea, the Eiffel Tower, represents one of the most extraordinary acts of creativity ever, and it ushered into being one of the great monuments to creativity ever built, so new at the time and yet still breathtaking almost 120 years later.

The Eiffel Tower is no more creative than satellites and space travel, medical breakthroughs and robot surgeries, digital strategies and social media. All represent the same theme, in that all were something very new at the time of their creation. All of them required the force of creativity for them to spring to life, and all of them disrupted the constant drone of common thinking.

"New" represents the impact of creativity, a bar set higher every time the status quo is breached, every time a creator visualizes something that has never been seen before. Whatever you call it, whether disruptive technology or innovative thinking, creativity is the inexorable force of progress, changing the landscape and the city skyline, encouraging technology shifts and innovations, and bringing out the best in us and what we could be.

CREATIVITY AS PERFECTED BY HIT SONGWRITERS

Hit songwriters provide remarkable and unique examples of how to use the creative gift. They return to the same deep well so many times during the course of their professional careers that they have to attune themselves to its exact location. Most successful songwriters write hundreds and hundreds of songs, at least, or sometimes thousands and thousands of songs, in the course of their careers. The path to their creativity has to be well worn, well lit, well protected, and well used. Inspiration is a given. Easy access to their creativity is a career necessity.

For most of my working life, other than that year I drove a taxi, I have had the privilege of knowing, signing, or working with a number of great songwriters. I have seen their creative geniuses in the best and worst of circumstances. I witnessed as they flew and as they stumbled, as they questioned their own ability one minute and took it for granted the next. But all had one thing in common—they could write a hit song.

Let's face it, anybody can write a song that *doesn't* connect. There are millions of those. There are songs written every year that will only ever matter to the person or people who wrote them. Only the gifted and rarest of songwriters can figure out a way to reach the public again and again, and make that public care about a little story that takes no more than three minutes to tell. Successful songwriters are truly among the most creative people in the world. They go into small, closed, dark rooms, often with nothing but their minds to rely upon, and emerge with intellectual achievements that inspire the rest of the world to act, whether to fall in love, stay up all night dancing, break up and make up with our girlfriends and boyfriends, cheer for our favorite sports team, or fight wars. Hit songwriters provide the music and lyrics that become the sound tracks of our lives out of little more than their intellect.

Songwriters do not enjoy creative superiority over other creators, but the frequency with which they must be attuned to their creativity is, by an evolutionary and career necessity, far greater than is the case for most other creators. Learning what they do most naturally can serve as a steady platform from which to discuss the process of creativity and how it can be managed as a method and practice for almost anyone else to use.

Lamont Dozier is considered one of the most successful songwriters of all time. He "listens to the world," as he describes it. He might hear a "phrase that pays" just walking down the street or while he's sitting in a restaurant, and he will drop everything to turn that idea into music. His method is uniquely his, and he is directly responsible for such hits as "Baby Love," "Stop! In the Name of Love," "I Can't Help Myself (Sugar Pie, Honey Bunch)," and several other #1 singles.

Hit songwriters are able to develop their own methods and processes, and have great success with the results. For this reason alone the rest of us should study them, their madness, and their remarkable ability at length, if we hope to achieve real and successful creativity in our own lives and pursuits.

Gaining an understanding of the varied approaches songwriters take, no one more correct than another, will serve to illustrate several techniques that can help you develop access to your own creativity. In the next chapter you will be inundated by this.

EXERCISES IN CREATIVE THINKING

What follows is the first of five exercises in creativity.

They are all designed to be "workouts" for the brain, encouraging new thinking and fresh ideas. You will be directed to ask questions to which you don't know the answers, to imagine what other people might do in the same situation you're in, to simplify your ideas until they are just onomatopoeias, and to imagine less common uses of common items.

The exercises are intended to exercise the brain, inspire the splashing of your neurons and their millions of synaptic connections, stretch out your acumen, and otherwise prepare your intellect to create new ideas. Possibly you will find a solution that is entirely different from any that have been considered before or, at the very least, discover new ways to look at old problems.

Hopefully these five exercises become valuable tools for you to use when starting a new project or trying to rev up your intellect to work on an old one. Or they may help when you're in a group creativity session that needs some tried-and-true warm-up drills. When the need for new and fresh ideas is upon you, these exercises will help you deliver. Please take a few minutes to try each exercise and experiment with the way you think, always demanding more from your brain.

Ultimately, if used correctly, the exercises will cause you to engage the most basic process of creativity—thinking thoughts that have never been thought before.

CREATIVE EXERCISE #1

The Excellent Question Game

❖❖❖

An Excellent Question is any question to which you do not know the answer. There's nothing more to it than that. This is not a game of riddles or a game of challenging your knowledge on any particular subject. This game is literally the opposite of Trivial Pursuit, in that you get rewarded only when you *don't* know the answer. This is a game about how to pursue *new* knowledge in an interesting way. So it's that simple: if you do not know the answer, it is an Excellent Question.

But then the game gets better. *There are no answers in the Excellent Question Game.* Only questions. Answers are boring and only muck things up, getting in the way of the momentum that will be created by all of the Excellent Questions. You never have to come up with any answers to any of the Excellent Questions you or any other players in the game ask.

This is an exercise for individuals or a group. I have played it by myself, with three friends at a dinner table, and in a lecture hall with more than five hundred students. It always works. This game stimulates one of the most important elements of creativity and creative thinking, and that is, of course, questions. Questions are a vital trigger for creativity. There is no creative process without them. After all, where would civilization be now if some hairy caveman, or more likely his hairy wife, did not pose the question, "What if we *cook* the bison, dear?"

I made a presentation on creativity at the Aspen Ideas Festival in 2011. To demonstrate how easy it is to think new thoughts, I asked everyone to play the Excellent Question Game. The subject was bees. Some of the questions they came up with were: How do bees make honey? How do they know where to go for flowers? How do they communicate with the other bees? Who decides which bee is going to be the queen? Why do they have stripes? Do bees have feelings? And then one gentleman asked if the queen bee was gay, which brought the room to a momentary standstill, and then a huge laugh. It was abundantly clear that the persons asking the questions did not know any of the answers, so all were deemed Excellent Questions.

When I changed the topic to the sun, the thinking of new thoughts continued. Some of the questions were: How far away is the sun? Is it solid? Will it ever go out? How much does it weigh? Does it make a noise? How close can you get before you melt? What is a sunspot? Did the earth break off from it? Was the sun once part of another sun that went supernova? Or was the sun the leftover molten core of some big planet that exploded? Again, since no one knew the answers, all were Excellent Questions.

Other topics might be: space, trees, water, dreams, music, love, the heart, weather, or the internal combustion engine. Almost any topic is a good topic for the Excellent Question Game.

As a way to inspire creativity, new thinking, and new thoughts, encourage yourself to ask more questions about everything you do and anything you see. Learn more about more things, and be in the habit of wondering how and why and who. Always ask one last question before a conversation ends. An inquisitive mind is a superb catalyst of creativity and a sanctuary for creative thinking, and it can better imagine things that are not there and events that have not happened yet, solving problems more readily by anticipating their impact and arrival.

As an example, say that a screenwriter is asked to write a screenplay about a new world far, far away. He has to imagine a universe in which he has never lived, and then populate it with people he has never known. He has to figure out how they got there, how they will survive, and how they will die. If he does not challenge himself and ask excellent questions, how does he figure out who is who and what is what? He asks himself many questions, and in the answers he finds the details he seeks about his characters and his story.

The Excellent Question Game is a starting point for curiosity, innovation, invention, and imagination. It is just an exercise at first, but it can quickly become a valuable tool for creative thinking.

CREATIVITY IN ACTION:
SONGWRITERS

IN THE PAGES THAT FOLLOW, YOU WILL MEET some of the greatest songwriters in the world. You will be presented with aspects of their creative process, describing the manner and method by which they are able to access and implement their creativity on a regular and systematic basis.

Yes, creativity is a gift, and either you have a lot of that gift or you do not. But whether you were endowed with an excess of this remarkable force or not, it does not mean you cannot gain better and more regular access to it. The tools that allow you to implement your creativity can be taught, learned, shared, and utilized as needed. These creators not only have the tools, but also the techniques and knowledge that allow them better management of thoughts and the thinking process. This allows them increased ability to recognize and be inspired by new ideas, and encourages them to be freshly innovative in every creative situation.

In 1990 Stephen Covey wrote a book called *The 7 Habits of Highly Effective People*. It has sold something near ten million copies and is an inspiration. Question: Is every reader suddenly as effective and successful and wealthy as the individuals storied about in the book? Very doubtful. But are readers confident that they will know better what to do in certain situations because they know what all of the "highly effective" people did in those same situations? Undoubtedly. Simply knowing what all of those other people did to become so effective is enough to help all of the "normal" people who read the book become more effective in their lives.

Similarly, these next pages are meant to offer you a range of possibilities from which you can choose when facing your creative tasks. You will be introduced to several highly creative people and learn some of their tools, techniques, knowledge, and processes. None are the same. All have found completely different ways to get it done. True, they are much more creative than most and prove this on a daily basis by earning their living as the elite in the elite field of popular songwriting. But what makes them so special is that they really do know what they are doing and, possibly more important, they know how they are doing it.

Who better to learn creativity from than someone who has the gift and knows how to use it.

ALAN AND MARILYN BERGMAN'S ART AND CRAFT

Alan and Marilyn Bergman are songwriters, creators in a very specific craft: lyric writing. They are best known for their songs written for motion pictures— "The Windmills of Your Mind," "How Do You Keep the Music Playing?," "The Way We Were," "In the Heat of the Night," and the score for *Yentl*—which have brought them Academy Awards, as well as Emmys, Golden Globes, and Grammys. They are also represented in the Great American Songbook by the songs "Nice 'n' Easy," "You Don't Bring Me Flowers," "Yellowbird," "That Face," and "Where Do You Start?" among others.

When asked about their process, they say there

are two things that inspire them—the film and the music. "The film is always the master," Marilyn says. "With the director and the composer, we discuss how the song is to function in the scene. The goal is for the lyric to seem part of the fabric of the movie, an extension of the screenplay." They will watch the film many times, in particular, the scene or scenes for which the song will be written. The composer will, perhaps, write several melodies and, together with him (or her), they choose the one that works best.

"The film and the music are the inspiration and then begins the perspiration," Alan says. "For us, the structure and shape of the lyric are found in the music, as are the rhymes. It's as if words are on the tips of notes and we have to find them."

Alan and Marilyn are not accidentally successful. They studied and prepared for their work. They were mentored by great lyricists long before they met each other—he, by Johnny Mercer; she, by Bob Russell. They learned the words of the great lyricists and the songs that make up the Great American Songbook. They analyzed the songs, asking themselves: "Why does that song last?" "Why does it still resonate and touch people?" "Why do singers still want to sing it?" The answer, according to them, "It's the music and what the song says and how it says it. It's how the song appeals to the heart and the mind."

Alan and Marilyn have been together for literally a lifetime. They have written lyrics with each other for so long that it is a seamless union, a mutual appreciation of each other and their ability, their art, and their craft. When one begins a sentence, the other can end it. They enjoy a shared sensibility of their professional challenges. Alan says, "We have two passions: We do what we love with someone we love. It's a wonderful life." They have mastered the art and craft of collaboration. It does not matter to them who wrote what. As they write, they are both creators and editors, and those roles change instantly. "Pitching and catching ideas" is how Alan describes this aspect of their process.

The study in their home is a sanctuary. It's quiet and peaceful. There's a piano in the corner and a view of the garden out the window. They keep a library there. Eight linear feet of books, filled with the works of the songwriters they most admire and respect, including Yip Harburg, Johnny Mercer, Irving Berlin, Cole Porter, Frank Loesser, Ira Gershwin, and Stephen Sondheim.

Many great singers have sung their songs. More than sixty have been recorded by Barbra Streisand, one of the greatest singers ever. Marilyn says, "We write for the human voice. If a lyric doesn't 'sing'—even if it is exactly what we want to say, exactly the word we want to use, we don't use it. That's where the craft begins. A lyric must feel good to sing." Marilyn describes the craft of lyric writing as the means by which she and Alan express their ideas. I asked, when is a song finished? She says, "When they take it away from us. As long as we have the time, we keep trying to make it better—writing and rewriting." Alan added, "And that's what separates the amateurs from the professionals."

Here are some more ideas about the creative process that we can take away from the Bergmans' practice:

- It's a mistake to fall in love with your words
- It's a mistake to think there is no other way to say something. There are always alternatives. It's a mistake not to explore them.
- There is something satisfying in a perfect rhyme—more satisfying to write, as well as sing, as well as hear
- Commercial success is *not* necessarily the only yardstick of creative talent
- It's best for a writer to be a reader—whatever is "grist for the mill"

- A lyric can change the character of a melody, and a single word can change the meaning of a lyric

They don't always know where a song is going when they start it, and oftentimes they do not know the title until the lyric is completed. But the Bergmans love to write. They love the journey, and the ultimate challenge of the empty page.

What we learn from these two professional songwriters, these two experts in the art of the lyric, is that nothing worth creating will happen simply as the result of a happy accident. "Accidental creativity" leads to one-hit wonders enjoying a brief moment in the sun, usually never heard from again. You might stumble onto something brilliant, but you cannot rely on a fortuitous phenomenon to build a lasting career path. If you do not know how you did it, you will never know how to do it again.

We learn from Alan and Marilyn Bergman that passion alone is not enough. It helps to know every square foot of the field of your endeavor; who preceded you on it, how they achieved the successes they achieved or how they failed, and why. Without knowing the history of your chosen art and its glorious past, you will probably not find your place in its future.

A BABYFACE RULE

Kenneth "Babyface" Edmonds is a songwriter, record producer, and magical live performer. His hits include #1 singles such as "I'm Your Baby Tonight" for Whitney Houston, "End of the Road" and "I'll Make Love to You" for Boyz II Men, and the ten-million-unit-selling sound track for *Waiting to Exhale*. He won the Grammy for Producer of the Year three years in a row. He formed LaFace Records (with L.A. Reid) and signed TLC and Toni Braxton as artists. He is a consummate music man, a recognizer of talent in others, and a truly creative thinker.

Thanks to Irving Azoff and Susan Markheim, my boss David Renzer signed Babyface to Universal Music, giving us the opportunity to drop in on his Hollywood recording studio anytime at all.

On one of these visits, Babyface said that ideas fly through his head at all hours, anytime, whether he is writing or reading, talking or sleeping. Some of them are brilliant, and some are not, just like with everyone who thinks of new things all the time. But what he does next is what makes him different from many other creators. He uses his memory as a filter. No matter how much he likes an idea as he is creating it, if he cannot remember it in the morning, he figures that no one else will, either. *And he lets it go.* He does not write down or record every thought he has, nor does he call his voice mail with every new melody or shout out to a secretary the intricacies of new lyrics. He does not try to preserve every single idea he comes up with. He lets the ideas stew. He is patient. He waits them out. At this point in his career he is interested only in writing hit songs, and one of the key markers of a hit song is that it be memorable. People need to hear it and remember it instantly so they can enjoy it even more the next time they hear it. This is what makes it a hit. It is sticky. The most successful popular songs are the songs that carry the most emotional weight, and the most memorable music and lyrics. These are the songs that people remember best. So if Babyface wakes up the next morning and cannot recall an idea with ease, he believes it may not have been such a memorable idea after all and was probably not a hit song to begin with.

Some of us are plagued by the ideas that appear briefly but then disappear just as quickly. These ideas are like phantoms, once seen but often never seen again. They sounded good at first, but now they cannot even be recalled. We will moan a midnight melody into a spouse's ear, or call our voice mail, or scratch a few words onto a pad placed next to the bed. But according to Babyface, that's all unnecessary. If an idea is any good, it will be remembered. If it's not, it will disappear beneath the waves somewhere, just like it was supposed to do. It might even be lost forever—right where it belongs.

Sometimes, the longer those forgotten ideas remain just out of reach, the more beautiful they become in our minds. Chastened in the memory, blushing and fleeting, and the next thing you know, the ghosts of all those forgotten ideas crowd the narrow boulevard where the new ideas are supposed to appear. Sooner or later, we see nothing but the ghosts, and our creativity is compromised.

If an idea cannot be remembered, it might not have been worth remembering.

The wisdom and genius of Babyface's rule is how it works in practice and habit, born of the way he partners with his intellect and the way he uses his creative process. He allows his intellect to serve as his filter, as his guard, preventing him from getting caught up in an idea that does not yet deserve his effort and focus. This guideline prevents fruitless searching of the intellect from getting in the way of discovering new thoughts.

SIR PAUL McCARTNEY'S
PERFECT PLACEHOLDER

Sir Paul McCartney is rightly considered one of the great live performing musicians in the world today, and he is certainly one of the world's great songwriters. He plays eight musical instruments, and sings while he plays them all. He wrote "Let It Be" and "Hey Jude" and "The Long and Winding Road" in addition to all of his collaborations with John Lennon as the founder, engine, and soul of the Beatles.

One of McCartney's greatest songs did not show up all in one piece, or even all at one time. The whole melody came first and then he had to wait weeks for the lyrics to show up. He said that he kept thinking it was too familiar to be original. In his biography, *Many Years from Now*, he writes, "I went round to people in the music business and asked them whether they had ever heard it before. Eventually it became like handing something in to the police. I thought if no one claimed it, then after a few weeks I could have it."

But to save the space for just the right lyric, one that would match the melody, he used a common and familiar phrase *as a placeholder* that took up the same amount of room and syllables and was easy to remember. The phrase, the placeholder, was actually the first-draft lyric of one of the most popular songs ever written. He sang "scrambled eggs" over and over in his melody, letting those words hold down the exact amount of lyrical space he needed, until he came up with something far better, far more memorable, and far more meaningful.

"Scrambled Eggs" ultimately became the Beatles standard "Yesterday." It is one of the most performed songs in the history of music. It has enjoyed more than eight million plays according to the performing rights organization BMI (Broadcast Music, Inc.), and it has been rerecorded (or covered) more than sixteen hundred times according to the song's publisher, Sony/ATV Music. It was named the greatest song ever written in a BBC radio poll in 1999. The world is a better place for having that beautiful song in it, and the song owes quite a debt to the placeholder Sir Paul used until the real lyric showed up.

Sometimes in the creative process, you will know the *size* of an idea that you want to use in a particular circumstance or situation—whether it is the exact number of syllables that would feel just right in a poem or song lyric, or the perfect size of a canvas that should be devoted to a particular image, or the length a jarring visual that should be on-screen in a documentary film—but you have not thought of the idea yet.

But the knowledge of what would be the perfect amount of space needed might arrive long before you know precisely what words or pictures or images will fill that space perfectly. This is where the placeholder is most valuable to the creator using it.

The placeholder holds down an amount of real estate, like someone saving seats at a movie theater while waiting for their friends to show up. It should capture the rhythm and gait of the phrase you want to write but have not written yet. Even if it feels entirely worn and ordinary and all too familiar, it does not matter because it is simply a placeholder and may have only the briefest little time to shine. It will exist only until the real thing comes along. Its purpose is to preserve the spot where an idea will fit in later, without interrupting or disengaging the creativity of the individual doing the creating. It may have a life span of a few minutes or hours, days or weeks, or, as in the case of "Scrambled Eggs," maybe a month or more. A placeholder's life span depends upon how long its creator needs to find the idea that will take its place.

A GERRY GOFFIN TECHNIQUE

The Brill Building was one of the centers of the song-writing and music publishing business during the late fifties and early sixties. The creative power that walked through those golden doors every day—writers like Phil Spector, Neil Diamond, Jeff Barry and Ellie Greenwich, Barry Mann and Cynthia Weil, Neil Sedaka and Howard Greenfield, Bert Berns, Leiber and Stoller, and many more—literally changed the world, and obviously for the better. Gerry Goffin and Carole King were among the most prolific and success-ful songwriters to emerge from the shadow of the Brill Building and I had the great privilege of working a little with both of them when I started out at Screen Gems.

They wrote a number of songs including "Will You Still Love Me Tomorrow," "Chains," "Up on the Roof," and "(You Make Me Feel Like) a Natural Woman," in addition to a surprisingly large number of other hits. But this story is about Gerry, who, later in his career, connected with Michael Masser and wrote "Do You Know Where You're Going To (The *Mahogany* Theme)" for Diana Ross, "So Sad the Song" for Gladys Knight, and "Saving All My Love for You" for Whitney Houston, along with many other hits. His is an extraordinary talent.

Gerry had been assigned to me as my writer, and my job was to find him writing collaborations and to get his unrecorded songs recorded. As I soon came to learn, he wrote only the lyrics and left the writing of the music and melody to his collaborators. As a result, he developed a somewhat off-putting technique for accessing his creativity. He sat with the music writer and let the melody wash over him several times, barely reacting to it at all. He told his collaborators to just keep playing the melody or the chord changes again, again, and again. It was as if he were meditating. One writer I had arranged to collaborate with Gerry, a talented musician named Jay Gruska, thought he might even have been comatose. He reported that Gerry's wife came into the room a couple of times and said, "Gerry. Wake up. Say something!" It may have appeared that he was sleeping, but he was actually far from it.

After lying there for however long he needed, Gerry would suddenly burst into creative splendor, and all in one go, like a sleeping giant coming awake, and he would fill a couple of pages with the first and basically complete draft of an entire lyric, top to bottom, without stopping—verse, chorus, bridge, verse 2, ad-libs—all of the words scribbled out on a lined yellow pad. The lyric came out of him like the devil at an exorcism. I saw him doing this more than a few times, and afterward he would look around the room like a magician having just completed his best trick. There were no rewrites, no revisions, no second thoughts—just his art, in the form of his lyrics, having exploded out of him.

Gerry knew that his creativity would be all the more successful if it all came from one state of mind, one moment of his intellect. If not, his focus could change gears abruptly and lose the point and purpose of his lyrical efforts. The magic could disappear completely. During the later stages of his writing career, he would also get bored and his mind would start wandering all over the place, so this process also served to get the most out of him when he did feel like writing.

Here's the wisdom from the Gerry Goffin I knew: Give yourself the freedom to capture the entirety of your creative efforts without stopping to nuance or edit the results. *Just let the whole idea out* unscathed. And out it will come, like a flash of light or a gust of wind. Allow your creativity to erupt from you, like an explosion, a burst of focused attention that lasts just long enough to allow the *entire* idea to emerge.

This technique will serve you well in the creation of almost anything, including a lyric, an article, or a book, the design of a bridge, the shape of a new building, or whatever creative task you have chosen to undertake. This does not replace a long, slow climb up the mountain of your creativity, nor does it give you a reason to circumvent all the hard work a project takes. Simply stated, this is one way to let your whole idea emerge—without edits or compromise. You sit and focus completely on your creative goal, almost meditating on it, and then, with a burst of energy, give in to the entire first draft of your idea, letting it explode out of your intellect. Quite possibly, like Gerry Goffin's bursts of creativity, it may just be a thing of beauty.

When songwriter Antonina Armato was just starting her writing career, and had been signed only a few months earlier, I offered her this technique. She, too, was challenged when it came to sustaining her creative focus for long periods of time. The method was a way to get the whole idea out before it was compromised by second thoughts. She adopted it immediately, and when she would tell me about a song she was writing, she would say, "I did a Gerry Goffin on this one. Tell me if you like it."

Now, years later, this "all at once" technique still serves as a key element of her process. She and her partner, Tim James, own Rock Mafia and call it

"GFN," or Good for Now when they complete the first draft of hit songs for Miley Cyrus, Selena Gomez, and many others.

This technique rarely fails, if you can give in to it. And while not every lyric will be a hit, every lyric will be *finished*, capturing the entirety of the thought it rode in on. It is thus an ideal tool for any creative project. Again, take your time, wait for the right moment, and only when you are completely ready, get it all done in one sweet moment, just like Gerry Goffin does. Long afterward, there will be plenty of time to sit back and marvel at the results.

SAY IT WITHOUT SAYING IT

Dennis Morgan is a Nashville songwriter who has been the BMI Songwriter of the Year three times and has written such outstanding copyrights as the worldwide hits "I Knew You Were Waiting (for Me)" and "I Wouldn't Have Missed It for the World," as well as the #1 country singles "Smoky Mountain Rain," "Years," and "Nobody," among many others.

It is like watching a master at work when he is around. And he is a perfect example of creativity unleashed. Dennis came of age as a writer and guitarist in the underbelly of the Nashville songwriter caste system. He arrived from Minnesota when he was twenty, with one hundred dollars in his pocket and a guitar in his hand. He soon found himself a job as a low-paid staff writer and studio guitarist. He would write songs all day, every day—often three or more writing sessions with different writers—and record the best of them in the evenings. As a result, practice became perfection and he became a very talented songwriter who knew what it took to put a great feel in the guitar part and a great hook in the melody of the songs he was writing. Malcolm Gladwell writes in *Outliers* about the necessity of a ten-thousand-hour apprenticeship in order to achieve greatness in a particular field. Dennis certainly had that time to give and willingly gave it, writing each day and recording each night, for years on end. This commitment was his apprenticeship. Yes, he had a prodigious talent, but it crystallized into a career because of the fact that he studied the best players, wrote with the best writers, worked with the best producers, and heard his songs sung by the best artists. In a town where success is measured by ASCAP and BMI Awards, #1 singles and Country Music Award "Hats," Dennis knows great success.

As of 2014, Dennis has written nearly *four thousand* songs and has had more than *one thousand* of those songs recorded and released. Not all songwriters are this prolific, of course, but he perfectly illustrates the concept of what an unlimited access to one's creativity can mean to a career. Like many successful songwriters, Dennis identified simple approaches to connect his life to his creativity, so much so that they are almost one. He is never *not* creating something. This allows him to find his creativity again and again, whenever he needs it.

One of the ways he guides his intellect is simple but so effective. He finds a different way to say something, different from the way he or any song he knows has ever said it before. This is how he challenges his creative instinct. If you bring him a hackneyed idea, he will reply, "Say it without saying it, baby. That's the only way we do it down here."

Say It without Saying It is one of Dennis's best tools to focus, access, and inspire his creativity. He follows this aphorism like it's a prayer. By using it regularly, he taught himself to be creative. He would reject ideas, his or anyone else's, that smelled of cliché, that he had heard somewhere before. He believes that continuing to root out the subtle and unique differences in language and musical phrasing will lead his creative instinct forward and improve the chances of catching a listener's ear. He believes this approach will allow him to tell the story that much more uniquely. The challenge sparks his mind into action—he cannot just run down the same road that he, or anyone else, has run down before. He is not the first songwriter to think of his creative art this way, but he is the one who described his process in a way that makes it so very understandable.

Dennis and I have worked together since I got into the music business. I tried to sign him to three different companies, but he turned me down each time and ultimately formed his own music publishing business, Little Shop of Morgansongs. Since I could not get him as a writer, I put him together with several of the writers I did sign, including Steve Cropper, Billy Burnette, and Simon Climie. Covers of his songs were frequent, including ones by Rod Stewart, David Lee Roth, and Aretha Franklin and George Michael.

Dennis believes that a creator has to search for new and better inspirations for his creativity, so that the results are his, and his alone, and that the ideas could be achieved by no one else but that writer. There is no joy for him in simply re-creating the obvious, that which has already been created. Thus he relies unfailingly on Say It without Saying It. It is part of his inspiration to keep moving forward, to keep creating.

The genius in the guidance of this rule is that it encourages creators to regard their subject matter and creative purpose differently every time they begin. Say It without Saying It. See what is *not* there. Imagine something *never* imagined before. Purposely and purposefully guide your instinct to think and create in the most original direction available and possible.

For all aspects of creativity, originality is vital. Whether building, cooking, curing cancer, or teaching children how to think, the success of any creative project is its innovative elements. Say It without Saying It will remind you to avoid clichés, dodge those dusty rhymes, think differently about everything, and challenge the purpose of your creativity just enough to inspire a significant measure of true originality.

THE LESS COMFORTABLE THE BETTER

Stephen Sondheim, one of the great theatrical musical songwriters in the world, described his first meeting with Leonard Bernstein. This was detailed in Sondheim's book *Look, I Made a Hat*. Bernstein was interviewing Sondheim to discuss the possibility of their working together to write a new Broadway musical, based on Shakespeare's great and most romantic play, *Romeo and Juliet*. The working title was *East Side Story*. Obviously the interview must have gone pretty well. The follow-on went just fine, and the results changed theater forever and gave the world one of its great musicals, *West Side Story*.

At this first meeting, Sondheim describes being escorted through Bernstein's Manhattan apartment to the "writing room." It turned out to be a smallish, cramped office that opened onto an air shaft in between the towers of the Dakota: no Central Park view, no picture windows, no plush comfy sofas—no extras of any kind apparently, save for a piano. It was just a place to think and work. Can you imagine this meeting? Two of the greatest minds in the history of theater getting together in a small room with no view, and in that room they would agree to write together works like "Maria," "Tonight," "I Want to Live in America," and all the rest of those master-pieces. It almost makes you want to stop everything you've been doing up until now and find a small, dark room somewhere.

It is not necessarily the case that intellectual cre-ation requires a comfy chair, a well-laid-out work-station, fresh and clean pens and pencils, a cup of warm cocoa with whipped cream, and some mint

Milanos. That may help sometimes, but only if the creator wants to make it look like he'd been doing some writing before he fell asleep. Creativity happens inside the head, not outside the body. Possibly hundreds of millions of synapses and neurons have to fire and splash all over each other just for one decent idea to even have a chance at life. Nowhere in the creativity manual does it say that extreme physical comfort helps in the slightest to achieve better thinking or more inspired efforts.

Build into the process of your creativity just enough physical discomfort and visual austerity to force your mind to make up the difference. By having little to see or experience when looking outside, you may well be inspired to find the beauty and art of your creativity looking inside.

PAUL SIMON'S USE OF RHYTHM AND REINVENTION

Paul Simon is one of the great songwriters there has ever been, or will ever be. Unlike everyone else mentioned in this chapter so far, he does not collaborate. He is his only cowriter. He has won twelve Grammys and written many of the greatest songs ever written, all alone. These include "Bridge over Troubled Water,"

"50 Ways to Leave Your Lover," "Homeward Bound," "Mrs. Robinson," "Kodachrome," "Mother and Child Reunion," and some two hundred others. He recently won the first-ever Gershwin Award from the Library of Congress in recognition of his creation of a remarkable catalog of songs. I attended a concert of his a few years ago and spent the evening awash in tears, realizing that almost every important event in my life was accompanied by one of his songs. When I went backstage afterward, he was gracious and genuine and everything you would hope one of your musical and creative heroes would be. He humbly shook my hand and softly thanked me for my kind words and compliments. I swear that I might not have washed that hand for at least a week. His drummer, Robin DiMaggio, was kind enough to arrange our meeting.

Paul Simon's is a beautiful genius: Mozart-like, unimpeded, a natural gift, as if this music simply fell out of the sky and into his lap. He finds melodies in unexpected places, and his rhythms accompany those melodies in unexpected and unforced ways. He uses the consonants in his lyrics as a significant structural support for his melodies, but the words sit so naturally in their spot that you cannot imagine them anywhere but there. It's almost like he is simply telling an interesting story, with rhythm and melody and harmony, not singing a song.

Sad but true, most creative genius shows up early, giving the creator confidence and license to try almost anything that occurs to him at any point in his creative life. Paul Simon's longevity is key to his creative freedom. He has been at it his whole life, and has written remarkable songs as a kid, an earnest young man, in a pop duo and as a solo artist, while slipping into middle age, and, as a legend, is still at it. But he is not the same writer now that he was then. His craft has matured along the way, and he has provided it with different avenues at the different stages of his creative life.

He said in an interview with Charlie Rose that he believes you are born with a reservoir of talent and that if you are successful, sooner or later you will use it up. That well will run dry and you will be tapped out. He believes you will then have to start over and re-create yourself. He has re-created himself musically several times. One way he achieves his reinvention is by borrowing the sounds and rhythms of other cultures and their music and incorporating those elements into his own music, particularly his songwriting. His career is dotted with hits and sounds, rhythms and beats, guitars and drums, and melodies from all over the world.

A three-hundred-year-old Mexican folk song called "El Condor Pasa" is the basis of his song "El Condor Pasa (If I Could)" from *Bridge over Troubled Water*. The haunting melody of a 250-year-old Lutheran chorale "O Sacred Head Now Wounded" by J. S. Bach, from his St. Matthew Passion, appears as the verse melody of Paul Simon's classic "American Tune," from the album *There Goes Rhymin' Simon*. The multiple-award-winning masterpiece that is his album *Graceland* was recorded primarily in South Africa and resulted in the first mainstream use of previously unknown world music beats, rhythms, harmonies, and instrumentation. Paul Simon thrived on the new sounds that were available to him, and used the grooves and beats to inspire songs like "Diamonds on the Soles of Her Shoes," "The Boy in the Bubble," and "You Can Call Me Al."

Fundamental to his continuously successful reinvention is his search for new rhythms to utilize in his songs and in the musical arrangements that surround them. He seeks out a new pulse, a new pattern, a new way to divide the symmetry of his beats, his lyrics, and his chord changes. He said, in the same Charlie

Rose interview, "The whole world responds to rhythm, and when the rhythm is right . . . they respond in a way that is just incredible . . . people jump up and they dance. It's a fantastic thing."

He went on to say, "Rhythm is an international phenomenon, but it is not a universal language." He allows himself to borrow freely and balance between the beats and rhythms from anywhere in the world to find those that most inspire his creativity. Every continent and culture has its own music, and he is unafraid to find the rhythms within them to set free his own creative efforts.

In a *60 Minutes* interview years ago, he said that for many years his songs often started with the rhythm while the music and lyrics came later. Since there are always new rhythms, somewhere in the world anyway, there are always more chances for him to reinvent and repurpose his musical ideas. Paul Simon uses new rhythms as an escape from the confines and complications of being a solo songwriter. The new sounds, new rhythms, and new beats are a way to bring new ideas into his creative system.

Anyone who wants more from their creativity can learn two key lessons from the life and life's work of Paul Simon.

First, invent and reinvent. Be open to anything

that might be a path to a new approach. Any inspiration will suffice. Every idea is a good idea. For Paul Simon, it was a sound or a beat, a harmony or a rhythm. For you, what will it be? If there is a chance to do so, try the path other than the one with which you are most familiar. It may inspire a whole new avenue of creativity, one you might never have known existed. Look for a chance to change what you do and how you do it. Think reinvention, not only of yourself and your creativity but of your process, too. Reinvention is just one path to manipulate your creativity and inspire your own personal innovation.

Reinvention completely changed the life of Pierre-Auguste Renoir, the painter. The story was told to me one night many years ago when my mother and I visited Jean Renoir, his son, the acclaimed filmmaker, and his wife, Dido, at their home in Holmby Hills. I had just been kicked out of the pre-vet program at UC Davis and was completely lost. When I told them what had happened, they related the story of Jean's father's journey as encouragement that nothing should ever stop me. He was first a painter of fine china. Only in his early twenties, after thousands of dishes, trays, and teapots, had he earned and saved enough money to afford his own paints and canvases—and reinvented himself as an Impressionist master. Or

Gustave Eiffel, mentioned earlier, who thought he was a bridge builder until he reinvented himself as a creator of landmarks by coming up with the idea for his famous tower, and shortly after that helped design the iron skeleton of the Statue of Liberty. Reinvention is a legitimate way to bring "new" energy and purpose to your efforts at creating.

Second, find the rhythm in whatever creativity you pursue and let it inspire you. Photographers may let the beat of a city inhabit the photograph they take of its skyline. Architects might allow the pulse of a hillside and the spill of the canyon below it to determine how the house will be built and what direction it will face. Novelists could let the steady drumbeat of the rain on their roof influence the pattern of speech in the characters they have created. Composers might let the waves pounding the seashore become the inelegant and irregular backbeat of a concerto or symphony. In whatever you pursue for your own creativity, let rhythm be one of the foundations of your creating, especially if it is a rhythm that is new to you, or just different enough from the rhythms you might usually make, to allow new challenges to find their way in.

Trust in these two central elements of Paul Simon's creative process and allow the creativity that results to be a new chapter in your creative life.

CAROLE KING AND BEING OPEN
TO CREATIVE INPUT

I was two months into my new job at Screen Gems–EMI Music when I happened across a Rolodex in the president's office that happened to have Carole King's home phone number on it. It was hard not to notice the orange markings that read EXTREMELY PRIVATE—DO NOT CALL. I immediately wrote the number down, raced back to my office, and called it before I had a chance to convince myself not to do something so crazy.

Sure enough, the card was right. It turned out to be Carole King's private number at her house in Idaho, where she was living with her husband and two young children. When she answered, I introduced myself and said I was new to the company and was available to her if she did not have another contact. She told me that she would love to work with somebody at her publishing company, but nobody had called her in almost ten years. I jumped right in and asked what she was working on at that moment. She told me she was in the middle of writing a song with her original cowriter and now ex-husband, the legendary Gerry Goffin. The song they were writing was called "Time Don't Run Out on Me." I knew plenty of people who were looking for great songs and asked her if I could hear it. She sounded a little reluctant but said sure and put the phone down on the piano. After a moment, she started to sing. Just for me, and only for me, a brand-new song still being created, still in process.

Please understand, I knew exactly who Carole King was. I *always* knew who Carole King was. From my earliest days figuring out who wrote the songs on my beloved Beatles albums, I read "C. King/G. Goffin" as the cowriters of "Chains" and never forgot. I knew that she also wrote songs for so many different artists, including Aretha Franklin, the Drifters, the Monkees, Little Eva, and Grand Funk Railroad. I knew almost every line of every song from her album *Tapestry*. I knew practically everything she had written. In a word, I idolized her and her sustaining ability to write hits songs. She was and is one of the great songwriters of this generation. So to hear her singing live over the telephone, in a private performance just for me, was astonishing.

Everything was going along perfectly, and I was having one of the greatest days of my life, and then something happened. That something was the bridge of her song. The bridge is supposed to be exactly that—a bridge, a musical idea that is neither the verse nor the chorus but explores the idea of the song in a new way, bringing you, the listener, back around to the chorus or refrain from a different angle. John Lennon said that you know you've heard a good bridge because it's the first thing you want to hear again when the song is over. Well, not in this case.

The song was remarkable and amazing, but . . . the bridge just was not. It was wrong for the song and I knew it the minute I heard it. When the song ended she picked up the phone, slightly out of breath, and said, "So what do you think?" I knew it was one of those moments, a moment I would never have again. I chose my words carefully and said, "Carole, if we are going to work with each other, I have to be able to be completely honest with you about your music and my reaction to it. It is the very least I owe you if you are going to let me into your world like that." She said a tentative okay and so I told her what I thought.

I told her that the song was great and that it took me on a wonderful journey, but that the bridge she had written was not perfect for that song, that it did not sound right, and possibly belonged in a different song. Then I held my breath. A long and silent pause followed, during which time it occurred to me that these might be my last few minutes in the music business. I had just called one of my new employer's most important songwriters, having nicked her phone number off the president's private Rolodex, and then practically insulted her songwriting and creativity. It would have been like getting a job with the Yankees, stumbling onto Derek Jeter's private number, and calling him to discuss his bunting in the late innings of close games.

Finally she said, "Okay, I'll think about it and let you know." We said good-bye pleasantly enough, but still . . . What had I just done? I raced into the office of the president, Lester Sill, and confessed everything to him. Soon his office was filled with executives wagging their fingers at me and asking me just what the hell I was thinking and who did I think I was. I suggested politely that everybody calm down somewhat until she called back, or didn't call back, and held out the possibility that everything would turn out just fine. I kept saying it, hoping to convince them and me. Maybe it'll turn out just fine. Maybe it'll turn out just fine. Maybe it'll . . .

Somehow, even though I knew very little about the business, I had faith in Carole King. She was a consummate professional in every respect, who came out of the songwriters finishing school that was the famed Brill Building (mentioned earlier). I knew in my heart somehow that she would be okay with a respectful challenge to her work. She would survive somebody telling her that a song could be better. This had been the role of others in her life, including music publisher Don Kirshner, who would tell her if he thought something she wrote wasn't strong enough to be a hit. I trusted in the fact that she would *want* to know if something did not work for her listener. I suspected that people had stopped telling her what they thought once she became a superstar.

A few days later the phone rang and my secretary announced the caller loudly enough so that they could hear her clearly downstairs at the EMI Recording Studio: "Tom . . . It's Carole King! On line two! Oh my GOD!" I picked up the phone and it was Carole. She said, "I thought about our conversation. I wrote a new bridge and I want to play it for you." She was very serious about the whole process, so serious it was almost solemn. And why shouldn't it be? We were treading on her most sacred ground—her creativity. I was under strict orders to let everyone know if she called me back, so by this time my tiny office was stuffed with executives, including Lester Sill, vice president of legal affairs Vince Perrone, head of operations Jack Rosner, and some other vice presidents. All of them had heard about her, of course, being that she was the company's most successful writer, but none of them had ever actually gotten quite this close to her or her art before. As soon as she put the phone down on the piano, back where it had been a few nights before, I put her on speakerphone. And when she started to play and sing, nobody moved and nobody breathed. It was that kind of a moment. There in my little office on Sunset Boulevard across from Hollywood High School, the world stopped spinning for a couple of minutes. The opening verses and choruses were just as beautiful as they had been the first time. And as the song progressed, all the execs were gesturing that I must be deaf or nuts or both to have sent her back to do some more work on this song. But for me it was all about the bridge.

So the song got to the bridge and I crossed my fingers. I hoped that I would love what she had done with it, and fortunately I did. She had taken out the fifties-inspired doo-wop bridge of the original and replaced it with a gorgeous and surprisingly emotional reflection that circled around and brought the song back to the first verse. It was much more honest and heartfelt and made the song basically perfect. At the end, Carole got on the phone and asked, "What do you think this time?" I shooed all the troublemakers out of my space and back to their own and told her how much I loved it, really loved it. And this was no lie; I did love it. I told her I would do everything I could to get the song covered, and fortunately, thanks to another executive, Judy Stakee, it did find a great home. The song was a #1 country single for Anne Murray about a year later. Go to YouTube and you'll find it. Look for "Time Don't Run Out on Me," by Anne Murray. And check out the amazing bridge!

Carole King accepted the creative challenge that had been presented to her by my comments—namely that the song might not be quite finished yet. She rose up to the challenge and rolled right over it, even though the opinion was only coming from some kid at her publishing company. I had no credentials, per se, no long trail of hits. I had achieved almost nothing and had nothing to base my opinion on but the fact that it was my opinion. But I had done something right. I had an honest reaction and was not afraid to share it. That in itself was what made the response real and the challenge genuine and obviously worth her responding to.

Just to be clear, Carole King did not need me or my opinions to finish her song. Would she have discovered the weaknesses in her bridge without me? Probably. Would she have taken the time to find the right words and music for that spot had I not said anything or called her that day? More than likely yes, but who knows? She was and is and always will be one of the great songwriters ever. My role that day was just to hasten her process in some small way.

When creating, be open to all creative input, to another point of view, to the reaction of your audience, even if it's only an audience of one. Enjoy a candid response to your creative efforts, an honest reaction to your song or story or artwork, a truthful reply to the question "So what did you think?" If you are unwilling or unable to welcome *all* the comments and suggestions that will arise, both positive and negative, you will miss out on several of the opinions and reactions that your creativity will inspire. The reactions are why you create in the first place. Adopt this step into your creative process and you can be much less precious about your art and ideas and much more open to the honest assessments that you will hear.

If Carole King, one of the great songwriters, can both request *and handle* an honest reaction to her art and creativity, then so, too, should any and every other person in the world who is, who wants to be, who dreams they can be, and who lives and dies to be more creative.

DIANE WARREN SHOWS UP

Diane Warren and I have been friends since we both started in the music business, back in the early 1980s. She had just written her first hit, "Solitaire," for Laura Branigan, and I was a brand-new song plugger. Back then, she was the most hardworking and dedicated songwriter anyone had ever met. Today, she is still the most hardworking songwriter I have ever met. Thirty years later, songs in her catalog have been recorded by many of the best artists in our business, including Beyoncé, Aerosmith, Toni Braxton, Celine Dion, Whitney Houston, Taylor Swift, and just about everybody else. She has been the ASCAP Songwriter of the Year six times. She has written eighteen #1 *Billboard* pop singles and has had more than fifty top 10 singles, and that's just in the United States. Overseas she is also one of the most successful songwriters. Albums that feature her songs have sold more than 350 million copies. She's also a brilliant businesswoman and, thanks in part to her remarkable father who believed in her when few people did, she owns the copyrights to all of her songs. The word "dedicated" does not even begin to describe her approach to her art and creativity, only because it completely understates the obvious.

She will have written at least a thousand songs by

the time she puts her pen down for the last time. While this proves the point that she has developed a ready access to her creativity, a career necessity for the successful songwriter, from that point on her process is the beneficiary of another gift—the fact that she is absolutely relentless. She is always working on something, and she never stops writing. There are no long breaks, there is no resting of the intellect, and there is no acceptable reason for her not to be either starting or finishing a song.

Her office is the same one she has occupied for the better part of three decades. She has expanded to now occupy practically the whole floor, but her writing room has never been upgraded. It's the same humble little mess it has always been, with lyrics all over the floor and a leaky window that she won't get fixed. The same dry-erase boards that used to note her covers for the year are still there, with the original song titles scratched on them. Here is "Un-Break My Heart" on one, and "I Don't Want to Miss a Thing" on another. And literally hundreds more. It's like being in the Diane Warren Museum.

And at 8:30 a.m. every day it begins, no matter what happened in her world the night before. At 8:30 a.m. on the six mornings after she was named ASCAP Songwriter of the Year, she was at her keyboard in her office on Sunset Boulevard. At 8:30 a.m. on the six mornings after she did *not* win an Academy Award for Best Song, she was at the keyboard in her office on Sunset Boulevard. At 8:30 a.m. on the morning after she *did* win a Golden Globe, finally, for "You Haven't Seen the Last of Me" from *Burlesque*, she was at her office working on something new. You get the idea. Hers is an unflinching and unstoppable pursuit of more, more, more. More songs, more hits, more recognition, more success.

What really drives Diane Warren? To my understanding, her creativity is her greatest passion. She finds joy, an absolute joy, being at one with it. They meet each other, day after day. She taps on the door where her creativity hides and is only at peace when it lets her in and lets her live, again. For her, it is the fresh idea, the new idea, the joy of a new thought, as well as perfecting the details of her existing ones. It is probably for this reason that she often considers her best songs to be her most recent songs. She will reach out to an A&R staffer, or other music executive, to pitch one of her songs, and say, "I want to play you a new song, the best song I've ever written."

When I called her to say I was writing a book on creativity and wanted to feature her in it, her answer was not unexpected. She said, "I'm in the middle of a song right now. Can we do it later?" I said, "Just tell me in a nutshell—in miniature." She said, "Okay, just say this. . . . Say 'Diane Warren shows up.'" And so she does.

Diane Warren's unrelenting daily approach to her creativity mirrors that of the great English writer and humorist William Somerset Maugham. When asked if he writes on a schedule or as a result of inspiration, he said, "I write only when inspiration strikes. Fortunately, it strikes every morning at nine."

Diane's daily mining of her intellectual possibilities requires constancy and a professionalism that few creators have. She is passionate beyond what most people will ever know, and as a result she has become one of the most successful songwriters in the world.

Wisdom from her experience? There is a great deal, but it is very simple. Show up every day. Create this morning like it's the last morning you have, like today is your final opportunity to say whatever it is you have to say. Show up and just keep showing up.

Sooner rather than later, your talent will emerge.

LAMONT DOZIER LISTENS TO THE WORLD

Lamont Dozier has been one of the most prolific hit songwriters in the history of pop music. His résumé lists fifty-four #1 singles to support this fact. Unlike some creators who need the room just so and the lighting just this way and the pencil sharpened just that much, Lamont has a much more open approach. He will accept inspiration from anywhere he can find it. When he wakes up, if he hears a bird chirping in the trees outside his window, he will put his tape recorder on RECORD and stick it out the window, recording the bird, listening for a melody that he can use that might be hidden in the chirping notes that the bird is singing. Sitting in a restaurant, he listens to the idle conversations going on around him—of couples and families and friends nearby—hoping for a snatch of a lyric or a couple of words never heard before, or a "phrase that pays" that might become the basis of his next song.

But he also listens to himself. He listens to the things he says during a conversation or a lecture, a new explanation of his skills, or an idea that just appears out of nowhere. He tells the story of when he was in a fight with his first wife and he had gone to stay at a motel so that she could have a day or two to calm down and remember how much she had loved him once not so long ago. She found out where he was staying and came after him, banging on the motel room door with an umbrella handle, her purse, her hands, whatever was handy. Certain that she would break the door down and cost him even more money, which he didn't have much of, he shouted out to her, "C'mon now, baby. Stop this. Just stop it right now. Stop, in the name of love . . ." With all that cacophony raging around him, the essence of a hit song presented itself. A few minutes later he had the outline of it in his head. That song, "Stop! In the Name of Love," became one of the most iconic of all the hits he wrote for Diana Ross and the Supremes. He also tells the story of his grandfather sitting in front of his grandmother's home beauty salon watching all the pretty girls come in and out of their house. His grandfather had a special greeting for each of them. One afternoon Lamont heard him say, "Hey, sugar pie" to one and "Hello, honey bunch" to another. It was not long after that when he was collaborating with his regular partners, Brian and Eddie Holland, aka the Holland Brothers. On top of the groove of a brand-new song, Lamont used what he had heard out in the world. And that's why the words "Sugar pie, honey bunch" begin the classic hit song "I Can't Help Myself" by the Four Tops.

He uses the same technique of listening to the world (and himself) when he is writing. He will sit at the piano and play and sing until something beautiful appears, whether a melody or a groove or a memorable progression of chords. But he then has to go back and figure out what it was. More than a few times I have seen him look up from a keyboard at the circle of admiring faces around him and say, "What'd I do? What'd I do?" Then he looks down at his hands and tries to remember what he did.

Creativity is any thought you've never thought before. But if you do not take the time to notice it, and do not make every effort to capture its beauty, it just may be lost forever. Now, according to Babyface, that would be proof that it was not such a great idea anyway, but that rule might not apply in every situation. Thoughts are ephemeral and fleeting things that alight like butterflies and disappear just as quickly if they do not find some recognition or refuge or happiness. The wisdom of Lamont Dozier and his creative process is that he is always on the lookout, always listening, always hoping to find it, and always ready to build a home for the next great idea that appears somewhere in his world.

THE CHALLENGE OF INSTANT CREATIVITY

For many years, Lamont Dozier and I were both governors and trustees for NARAS (National Academy of Recording Arts and Sciences), the organization that awards Grammys and facilitates "music's biggest night." As part of those responsibilities, he and I worked closely together giving lectures on creativity at several Grammy Camps—gatherings of local high school students meeting songwriters, executives, and other people in the music business. Those lectures were the first steps of writing this book.

Lamont is remarkably comfortable with his ability to listen to an idea from a collaborator and then instantly turn it into a song, practically at will—so comfortable that he let me try an experiment one year. I asked him to help me with the presentation, but then to write a song on the spot, without any time to prepare. He said of course and that he was looking forward to the challenge. To make it all the more interesting, I invited Keri Hilson and Sean Garrett to join us. Keri's biggest hit is one of my favorite modern pop songs, "Knock You Down," featuring her with Kanye West and Ne-Yo. Sean Garrett wrote for Ciara, Nicki Minaj, and Beyoncé, but is best known as one of the writers of Usher's "Yeah."

The first half of the lecture went very smoothly. It was all about creativity and the three writers shared numerous insights and stories of their careers. The crowd was approximately 250 students, rapt, silent, and totally engaged. But then came the magic. I told the unexpecting audience that they were now going to see all of that wisdom come to life before their eyes, because Lamont, Keri, and Sean had agreed to write a new song, right there, right then, right in front of them. And they had agreed in advance that the audience could give them parameters for rhythm, tempo, lyric content, and the artist they should write for.

The room was instantly buzzing, and it wouldn't stop. I knew that none of the students had ever seen anything like this before, because nobody had ever seen anything like this before. Lamont and I had come up with this idea only a few days earlier. By a show of hands, the students asked for the song to be midtempo, to be a duet for Beyoncé and Usher, with the subject of the lyrics being how great love used to be but was not so much like that anymore. The next thing you know, that room was flying away into the cloudless unending sky of Lamont's, Keri's, and Sean's creativity.

Lamont started picking out chords on the piano, hinting at melodies, establishing the basic groove. Keri heard something she liked in his performance and started to riff on it. Sean soon found his footing and then, in about three minutes, *it was on*.

Completely out of nowhere, with nothing but their will and willingness to carry them, these three remarkable writers crafted an instantly powerful song, with verse and chorus, intro, and even a little bridge. It was rich and full and passionate. It was rough around the edges, yes, but still it was perfect. It was the kind of thing you always wish you could see: writers actually writing a song together. I was practically holding my breath as I watched. Just a few minutes later, when they all caught one another's eye and sang the final note, the room exploded. The applause and cheers would not stop. It was extraordinary. I have it posted on my website. Take a look—it's practically magic.

Lamont, Keri, and Sean all completely trusted in the process, in their own instincts to create, and in each other's artistry. No one was afraid to share an idea or to see it fail—and possibly that's why they succeeded so brilliantly. There was not time to hesitate, with a couple hundred kids holding their breath and watching. It was instantaneous and exciting and chilling to see the raw power of their collective intellect pushed to the edge, and the results being such a perfect little pop song. I wish I could tell you that the song was recorded and became a huge hit, but that has not happened yet.

To me the lesson of that incredible day was that

creators have to completely trust their ability to create, no matter how unusual or uncomfortable the setting might be. They have to love the *new* of any situation they find themselves in and allow that challenge to be a further point of inspiration. They must be ready at almost any time to welcome an opportunity to exercise their creative strength and power.

And who among us has not found herself or himself in a difficult situation where the only way out was a burst of creativity? Not creativity prepared and fretted over so that every last detail is perfect. Not fresh from the oven. Just needed, whether to save a life or save an evening. Sometimes there is time for only a bit of instant creativity. If you find yourself there, trust in your ability. And then leap in.

SIR GEORGE MARTIN ON THE EARLY BEATLES

Sir George Martin is a living legend. He is widely considered to be one of the great record producers ever. He was the discoverer of the Beatles, and the original producer of their untouchable recordings. He was also the principal creator of the orchestral arrangements that accompany the Beatles' catalog, as well as the architect of their renowned vocal harmonies.

George Martin was the executive who had the prescience to sign the Beatles to their UK record deal in the first place, and his signing of the band to EMI Music is considered the best signing of any artist in the history of the music business. I was president of Chrysalis Music Group in the 1990s and Sir George was on the board of our parent company. He had come to Los Angeles to raise money for his charities and to introduce a lecture he had prepared on the making of *Sgt. Pepper's Lonely Hearts Club Band*. Every chance I had with him, I tried to turn the conversation to the Beatles, their writing, the recording techniques he used, their creative process, anything at all about the band I have always considered to be the most important event that ever happened to pop music.

One day at lunch, he was talking about the band members very early on in their careers, when they were new as writers, new to the creative process, new to recording, new to everything. But, according to Sir George Martin, Paul McCartney and John Lennon had already reached an agreement between themselves about their songwriting. They had agreed, implicitly or explicitly, he did not say which, to show complete respect for each other's creative efforts, as evidenced by two facts. First fact, that every song would have both their names on it, as equal creators, regardless of which one of them wrote the song, and regardless of the percentages of credit. There are several songs for which they share writer credit that clearly only one of them wrote, such as "Yesterday" and "Let It Be." Second fact, and more important for this discussion, was their agreement to *not criticize each other's ideas*, but instead, to try to write the next part of the song that much better. Imagine, even at the very beginning stages of their world-changing careers, they understood on some innate and spiritual level how vital it was to show each other's creativity distance and freedom. Instead of an aside about one's verse or chorus, intro or bridge, the other tried to write the next part of the song even better. If one of them happened to write a verse that was not spectacular, the other one would write an amazing chorus that was. If one arrived with a song that meandered through the verse into the chorus, the other might try to write a spectacular bridge to offset it. As their careers progressed, John and Paul began to write many more songs as individuals and fewer as collaborators, but the rule of complete creative respect still held. If John wrote a song that Paul did not particularly like, Paul would then write a song of his own and try to make it better than John's. The rule stayed in place and was apparently an accelerant in their creative process, and how could it not be? They were each competing with and against the other best songwriter in the world.

The wisdom of this one aspect of the Beatles' creative process is pure and undeniable. Criticism is an idea killer. A naked criticism, especially from someone who is close, can completely stop the flow of an idea faster than a bucket of cold water poured over someone's head. A wince, a grimace, and even just a dismissive shake of the head are pure poison, especially to very new ideas. These kinds of responses show lack of faith in the ultimate outcome. Snap judgments, especially in the negative, are purely unkind and have no place in a successful working collaboration.

When collaborating, why not adopt this same simple and genuinely respectful policy toward each other's efforts? Avoid the urge to criticize. Skip the first thing that comes to mind, unless it's positive. Allow your collaborator the chance to fly and fall, to swing and miss, to feel the freedom to explore every idea. If an idea is completely unworkable, that will become apparent to everyone, but in the meantime show each other's creativity complete respect. Find your inner Beatle and make the other person's ideas better by improving on what comes next.

While discussing Sir George Martin's permanent place in music history for signing and producing the Beatles, it would also be fair to mention an individual who played a crucial role in the success of the band in America, and without whom, who knows what would have happened. That was Alan Livingston, president of Capitol Records in the early sixties, who proved himself to be one of the most visionary executives in the music business, now or then.

Livingston was a creative enabler, giving many great musicians opportunities they otherwise would not have had. After George Martin signed the Beatles to a UK-based deal, it was Capitol Records' option to pick up the rights to release their albums here in America. Livingston quickly exercised that option. He then purchased the rights to singles that had already been released by several different independent labels, consolidating Capitol's hold on the band. He saw that the act was about to explode and gave their releases complete priority throughout the company's marketing and promotion divisions, resulting in the Beatles having the top five songs on *Billboard*'s pop chart one memorable week. But most important, Livingston was the one who paid for them to fly to New York to appear on *The Ed Sullivan Show*, the performance that turned them from a new band into a phenomenon. Livingston obviously had a great ear for talent. During his tenure, Capitol Records also signed the Beach Boys and Frank Sinatra. Livingston helped design the Capitol Records tower (to look like a big stack of 45s), and was the creator of Bozo the Clown. Later, as a top TV executive, he was responsible for green-lighting the fourteen-season western *Bonanza*. All that *and* the Beatles. Thank goodness for Alan Livingston.

REGINALD DWIGHT'S GREAT DISCOVERY

At seventeen, Reginald Dwight was a London-based musician much in demand, and his band Bluesology was a regular backup outfit for American bands and singers playing in London, such as the Isley Brothers and Patti LaBelle. He tried out as the vocalist for several bands, including King Crimson, but was never chosen. He then answered an ad in a music magazine. It had been placed there by UK record executive Ray Williams, who was looking to discover new songwriters, and potentially introduce them to one another. This is how Reginald Dwight came to know the person who changed his life forever, another creator, someone who was as good at writing lyrics as Reginald Dwight was at writing music.

The world of music changed that day, and it is different because of that ad and what Williams did when he heard the creative efforts of the two writers. The lyricist was Bernie Taupin. And it was his ability with words and storytelling that allowed Reginald Dwight to give up writing lyrics completely and forever and become Elton John. Fundamental to his transformation was the realization by Reginald Dwight that he was better off writing the music, leaving the writing of lyrics to someone who could write lyrics as well as he could write music. In a very short time, the onslaught of hit songs that made his career began to appear. Songs like "Levon," "Your Song," "Rocket Man," "Honky Cat," "Daniel," and "Crocodile Rock." And then appeared a staggering work, a towering double album that many people, rock critics and fans alike, consider one of the best pop albums ever: *Goodbye Yellow Brick Road*.

From the very beginning of their collaboration, when Ray Williams handed him a stack of Bernie Taupin lyrics, Elton has trusted in the genius of his lyrics writers, and never changed a word of a song that was put in front of him. *Goodbye Yellow Brick Road* was no exception. According to the album's producer, Gus Dudgeon, speaking in an interview for Claude Bernadin's book *Rocket Man*, Bernie Taupin wrote all of the lyrics over a two-week period and sent them en masse to Elton, who wrote all of the songs in one unbelievable three-day stretch. The recording took place in France at the same studio where Elton had previously recorded two albums. The writers never saw each other during the writing and recording process. They were never in the same room, never heard or saw each other working. There were no suggestions or judgments. Bernie lived outside the recording process and he wrote all of the lyrics prior to hearing a note of a melody. And what lyrics he came up with, for "Goodbye Yellow Brick Road," "Candle in the Wind," "Bennie and the Jets," "Harmony," "Love Lies Bleeding in My Hand," and "Saturday Night's Alright for Fighting"—twenty-two songs in all, each perfect in its own right, each created without the collaborators ever collaborating. Complete trust by each man of the other was required, or this remarkable collection would never have found its way into the world. The album is about to celebrate its fortieth anniversary, and was recently inducted into the Grammy Hall of Fame.

Elton does not stand in judgment of his writer's lyrical art; he lets it live and he lives within its boundaries. He trusts his collaborators completely, like a skydiver with his parachute. Elton never changes a word of a lyric—in the same way that Alan and Marilyn Bergman never change a note of the melody—and this maxim applies to all of his lyrical collaborations. Bernie Taupin was the lyrical heart of Elton John, the artist, and together the songs they wrote helped Elton sell in excess of two hundred million albums. When Elton shifted his creative focus to write musicals for film and Broadway, he found other collaborators. But the key element of his creative process did not change. He continued to trust his lyricists completely. He wrote *The Lion King* and *Aida* with Tim Rice, and, according to his manager, Johnny Barbis, never changed so much as a syllable of "Can You Feel the Love Tonight," "Circle of Life," and "Hakuna Matata." The same parameters held true when he wrote with Lee Hall for the musical adaptation of the film *Billy Madison*. Elton found something that works for him and he has not wavered from it, in forty years of successful hit songwriting.

Reginald Dwight's great discovery was that he was *not* something, particularly not a lyricist, and that he would never be as good with words as he was with music. He was brilliant to recognize that he would never be a phrase-smith or title-man like Bernie. He somehow arrived at the conclusion that someone else's genius was equal to, or possibly even greater than, his own. Had Reginald Dwight not accepted this great revealing truth about himself, the world would never have known Elton John and all of those amazing songs.

Elton John's story provides much wisdom regarding teamwork and creativity. In your own collaborations, if you are working with someone who is great at something, trust that greatness. Accept their gift and do not question it. Let it lead you. If you can, turn an honest eye on yourself, look to see what you are *not* great at, and find someone who is as great at your weakest link as you are at your strongest. Reveal to yourself what you will never accomplish and find someone who can accomplish it.

For this to work, it is vitally important that you know what you do well and what you do *not* do well, so you can find a partner who makes up the difference between what you are and what you are not. Recognize where you end and where somebody else begins. Let the sum of your collective creativity be greater than your individual efforts alone would be. Let the best of both sides meet somewhere in the middle, and each of you will fulfill what is missing in the other.

If you are Elton, look for Bernie. If you are Bernie, find Elton.

CLIVE DAVIS AT HIS MOST CREATIVE

As will be discussed in detail later on, the physiological process of creativity, the brain's workings and renderings, is the same process regardless of the output of that particular brain. The "machine" of the brain will operate as designed regardless of what it is asked to create: blood flows, neurons fire, synapses connect them, a mist of excitatory spray assists, and we call it thinking. But *what* gets imagined and *how* it gets imagined are as different as are snowflakes and raindrops. As many ways as there are to imagine is how many ways there are to create. Some of us write lyrics or poetry, speeches or screenplays. Others hear music in the stars. Some set their muse free in order to create fashion or marketing campaigns for bubbly beverages. But the physical process does not change.

When I heard Clive Davis describe the situations in which he is at his most creative, it took me by complete surprise. We were sitting onstage at the Roxy Theatre in Los Angeles in front of a sellout crowd of more than four hundred of his admirers.

It was a public conversation to benefit MusiCares, a Grammy charity, and my role that night was to ask good questions and stay out of the way of his answers. Clive was on a tour promoting his stellar autobiography, *The Soundtrack of My Life*, which had just become a *New York Times* bestseller.

Clive is one of the most successful music executives in the history of the music business. His companies have sold literally hundreds of millions of albums and CDs, and about half as many singles. He has signed and discovered or worked with a who's who of music business legends, including Janis Joplin, Whitney Houston, Aretha Franklin, Patti Smith, Carlos Santana, Barry Manilow, Alicia Keys, Simon and Garfunkel, Bruce Springsteen, and countless others. He signed LaFace Records, put Sean Combs into business, and gave Jive Records its first opportunity in America. He founded Arista Records and sold his interest in it twenty-five years later for hundreds of millions of dollars. To this day, in his seventies, he still oversees the creation of recorded music at Sony BMG as CCO (chief creative officer) and insists on being part of every detail of the marketing and promotion efforts of his projects as well. He is a Harvard Law School graduate, a multimillionaire, and a mentor to everyone who asks. In addition, he is also supremely focused and is both a great businessman and an extraordinary discoverer of new and raw talent. No, he's not a songwriter, but he is probably the best friend a songwriter could have: he is always listening for great songs and always recording them.

I asked him a lot of questions that night, one of which was: "When are you at your most creative?" I was expecting almost any answer but the one I got. After a moment to think about it, he said quietly, "When I listen." I was dumbfounded. I had never heard someone describe achieving their creativity that way. Writing, composing, drawing, painting, designing . . . yes. But listening? Never.

Over the years then, I guess I have seen him at his most creative hundreds of times because I have played him hundreds of songs. He glances at the lyric sheet in front of him, and completely focuses on the job at hand . . . sometimes closing his eyes as he decides if a song has what it takes to be a hit record. He prefers if you do not tell him who *you* think should sing the song you are playing. His roster of artists usually runs about three pages, so he likes to make the connection between artist and song without any prompting.

Almost all of the time he tells you what is wrong with the song, and why it misses the mark, and what would have to be done with it to make it right for the artist he's thinking of. And every once in a great while, he looks up and smiles and says, "I love it." He said this to me when I played him a song by Dennis Morgan and Simon Climie called "I Knew You Were Waiting (for Me)." He was looking for a duet for Aretha Franklin and George Michael, and he found it in that demo. The song was recorded shortly afterward. When it was released, it reached #1 on charts all over the world, and won Aretha one of her record-setting eighteen Grammy Awards. Believe me, it was one of the great meetings.

Clive does not write lyrics or improve melodies. He does not come up with significant arrangement ideas or background vocal parts or mixes. He does not play any musical instruments at all, nor does he read music. Yet he is considered one of the most creative executives the music business has ever known. Why? Here's what I think: He has mastered the language of creativity and the nuances of communicating what he wants to hear in a song or recording he is working on. The best songwriters, producers, artists, and musicians in the world will do whatever he asks of them. That might mean rewriting a section of a song, or remixing a final master. When he listens—that is, when he creates—he judges and assesses the creativity of others and the likelihood of that music, those songs and these recordings, gaining real popularity with an ever-changing and very fickle public. His creativity blooms when he listens to a song. He responds to it emotionally and intellectually, and then speaks on behalf of the artist's fans regarding whether or not it will be a hit. More often than almost anyone else in the business, he is right. He hears what no one else seems to be able to hear.

DR. DRE'S BEAT ROOM

The producer in music is like the director in film. He's the boss. He's the one getting paid cash plus points. He's the one who tells the singer how to sing and the musicians how to play. He supervises the mixing and mastering. He is the captain of the ship, and the one to whom most of the credit will go (in the case of a success), or most of the blame (in the event of a grand failure). All big decisions that result in what you hear when you hit PLAY start and end with the producer.

One of the best, most significant, and most revolutionary is Andre Young, also known as Dr. Dre. He produced many of the most important early West Coast hip-hop records, by artists like N.W.A, Ice

Cube, and Eazy-E. He cowrote and produced "Nuthin' but a G Thang" from his own album *The Chronic*, and then produced the debut album for Snoop Dogg, *Doggystyle*. Soon after that, he started his own company, Aftermath Entertainment, and immediately signed an unknown white rapper from Detroit named Eminem. Eminen and Dre cowrote, and Dre produced, the breakthrough single "My Name Is." Then, in partnership with the Slim Shady label, Dre signed 50 Cent and cowrote and produced "In Da Club," the biggest-ever hip-hop single. He has won Grammys for Album of the Year and Producer of the Year. He has continued to write and produce and, most recently, founded (with Jimmy Iovine) the hugely successful Beats by Dre headphone business.

Maani Edwards and I signed 50 Cent to Universal Music, thanks to a tip from my secretary Cory Bergen, whose brother heard "In Da Club" at a frat party. During the course of the pursuit of 50 Cent, we heard a lot of stories about how the album's production was going, and that's when I first heard about a "beat room." But in the supersecret and ultra-competitive world of hip-hop, no one would share the details of how it worked, or even where it was. But even so, it sounded amazing.

Shortly after that, I signed a writer/producer, beat maker, composer, and keyboardist extraordinaire named Mark Batson. He had been building his catalog by working with artists like Seal, India. Arie, and the Dave Matthews Band, but had also worked extensively in the beat room alongside Dr. Dre, making tracks for numerous projects, including for 50 Cent's and Eminem's albums. I could finally talk details with someone who had actually been there. Mark shared what it was like sitting in with one of the legendary producers in the music business, and how it was a different process from any other situation he had ever been in. He said, "You go into that room like you are walking into a sonic spaceship. The studio is *Star Trek*, and you are in search of this magical thing that can only be found in that room. It is the *Enterprise*.

"So in the room, it's a line of people, could be two or six depending upon what Dre's looking for, what record is being made, what artist is next. Each player has a bank of beat machines, drum machines and keyboards, and hundreds of sound selections available to them. The massive sound libraries allow for practically unlimited combinations. But if you play an instrument, you can bring that, too. In addition,

Mike Elizondo is a bass player and producer who often joins Dre's sessions.

"No matter how many players, all the machines are wired to play through two huge studio monitors at the front of the room. Everyone's sounds are rough-mixed together, all coming through the same way. It becomes a beat orchestra. He'll start it with a kick drum—the pulse, the driving force. The other musicians then contribute what they think makes it happen.

"He always starts from scratch. And restarts from scratch. If it's not happening, he'll stop and start again. Most beats get rejected. Out of all the beats that come out of the sessions, only the 'most right' get to the artists, especially someone like Eminem.

"Dre searches for inspiration from his team, and then provides that inspiration to the artist who'll write the lyric and the fans who'll live because that song is their lives.

"He'll isolate a sound that's bigger than all the rest and say 'great' and everyone else stops until the perfection of that sound is leading the band, and then the others play along with it. It's competitive. If someone creates something that Dre loves, there is a push among all the others in that direction. It's a team effort, but more like a team of all-stars—where the bar is set very high. Players will shout out to each other, 'What was that, what was that?' when someone plays something amazing, and the whole room reacts to it, shouting, 'Get that down, that's it!' The beats and hooks are like the words and lyrics you might hear in other situations.

"Dre aims only for perfection. On a scale of one to ten, he is only looking for twelves and thirteens. And he won't stop until he finds it. Dre is a leading expert in the sound of timeless club music, timeless car music. 'Cause he's patient. A perfect beat could take an hour, two hours, three years, or fifteen minutes."

Mark Batson's description of Dre's creative process is so clear and understandable it's like a portrait of the man. Here's what else I got from it: First off, Dr. Dre's Beat Room is the essence of why people are *in* the music business. It is there to create, to most purely just create. It is in a recording studio in the San Fernando Valley, located on the same piece of Ventura Boulevard that Tom Petty sings about in "Free Fallin'." Thousands of people drive by it every day having no idea what goes on there, yet it is ground zero for one of the most consistently significant and creative producers in the game. Most of these same people have never even heard of it, although almost all of them have heard music *from* it—if they listen to hip-hop, that is, and if they listen to where hip-hop has been and where it is going, and if they listen to the best and most creative producer's music.

Second, Dr. Dre creates only new music, that is, is at his most creative, when he is surrounded by great musicians who are *competing* with him to make the best sounds, beats, grooves, and magic any of them have ever heard before. He chooses the best of their contributions to blend with his own into the perfect beat, encouraging them and feeding off them at the same time—to inspire himself.

I never heard of anyone who got it done like this, until Mark provided all those remarkable details. Unlike Elton John, who finds collaborators who do what he *cannot* do, Dr. Dre finds people who do *exactly* what he does. He fills his creative space with other beat makers, armed with the very same quality of equipment and library of sounds to choose from, like an armory. He competes with them, pushes them for more and better and perfection, seeking out the best of their expertise and artistry to inspire him to make the most of his.

And unlike Diane Warren, who prefers to start each day alone and create in the peace and vacuum of her small, quiet writing space, Dre never works alone. And it's never quiet. And it's not that small, either. His room is more like a semiorganized rhythmic free-for-all in a bounce house. Six players plus engineers, and everyone has plenty of space in which to operate. The more noise and grit and passion the better. Dr. Dre thrives on this—the music, and the competition to create it—and supervises the cacophony of beat making that goes on there. It is a carousel of planned yet accidental collisions of sound, creating tracks that will have a chance to be a part of the future of music.

What do you take away from all this? Most important, know who you are and how you create most effectively. Build an environment around you that allows for the best of you to emerge with the least amount of resistance. Try anything that might work for you, whether it is a room full of quiet comforts or rowdy drinking buddies. Competition for inspiration may not be such a bad thing in a setting like this one. There is no *one way* to create. There is only the way that works best for you. You have to discover it, then refine it, and keep refining until it's perfect (for you).

Dr. Dre quite obviously knows himself. Do you know you?

CREATIVE EXERCISE #2

If You Were Someone Else, How Would You Think?

❖❖❖

This is an exercise in looking at a creative challenge from different angles and points of view. It encourages you to imagine how others would respond to the same insurmountable obstacles you might be faced with during the course of your creativity. Here's how it works.

First, pick a challenge, any challenge. For the sake of the exercise make it one of these three: a) Write a speech to be given at the UN on global warming; b) Design a memorial to honor fallen hero firefighters; c) Organize a fund-raising evening at a school for the deaf that includes interactive electronic live performances.

Second, pick a someone. Possibly Steve Jobs, Warren Buffett, Maya Angelou, Mark Zuckerberg. Or U2's Bono, Justice Sonya Sotomayor, Bill Clinton, or talk show host Chelsea Handler. You have also just met several extraordinary creators, any one of whom might be a good candidate, as well.

Third, combine a challenge and a someone. Try to imagine what these individuals would do with one of the creative challenges noted. Warren Buffett's speech on global warming would be far more dire and much less spiritual than Maya Angelou's, for instance. Clinton's fund-raising efforts would have more flash and Chelsea Handler's would have less substance, for instance. Not to say that one would be more successful than another, just different.

This exercise encourages you to discover what persons other than yourself might utilize to solve a problem or what they might bring to find a solution in any creative situation. How would they sneak up on the issue you are trying to make sense of?

This is also an exercise in looking at an idea, any idea, differently. And this may just be the step you need in order to, say, finish your screenplay, or capture a photograph that speaks a thousand words, or craft a new worldwide campaign for beer, or whatever it is you are working on.

There are no wrong answers, of course, but the search for the thoughts and ideas that others might use, or an action they might take in any given situation, is one way to look at an idea with new eyes. As a result, you will likely come up with a very different perspective than you would have without trying this exercise.

CREATIVITY AND HISTORY

"S URVIVAL OF THE FITTEST" IS A TERM created by Charles Darwin in his great work *On the Origin of Species*. But maybe it wasn't just the fittest who survived; maybe it was also the most creative. Mark Tramo believes that some form of creative acumen had to exist to set humans apart from other animals and that it lies at the core of our evolutionary success. "Creativity became part of our genetic endowment and it has helped us survive; creativity is a 'selected for' trait."

Suppose the earliest humans hunted more successfully because they were able to imagine more accurately where their prey was headed or hiding. Suppose this was the ability that led to the survival of this particular line, which leads to us now. A strong imagination is a force of creativity.

Or even earlier. What about the first of our ancestors who stood up straight and grabbed a discarded bone to use as a weapon against his enemies? That must have been a brand-new thought he or she had never thought before. New ideas are a product of creativity.

In a few pages you will read about a group of our immediate forebears who painted on cave walls the stories of their lives. These are believed to be the first-ever examples of narrative storytelling by man. Storytelling is a process of creativity.

Creativity has been one of the most desirable, most coveted and revered, and least understood human traits as long as there have been humans. While there is a great deal of science devoted to it, still so little is known about creativity and its origins. We have always known it existed, in one form or another, but for many centuries we just did not know what to call it when we saw it in one another.

According to *Collins English Dictionary*, the word

"creativity" itself did not even make its first appearance until 1870 or 1875. Most ancient cultures, including that of the ancient Greeks, did not even have a concept of creative thought. We have come a long way.

So what follows here are several examples of creativity as practiced and developed in the lives and minds of several great creators, some of them practicing their art long before the word "creativity" even existed.

THE CAVES OF LASCAUX AND THE FIRST KNOWN STORYTELLERS

Inside a series of caves in southwestern France are among the earliest known examples of art, storytelling, and of the importance given to preserving the human experience, in other words, of creativity. The art that has been discovered on the walls in these caves represents the first time, as far as we know, that man ever bowed down to his own creative instinct as a deliberate act, the first time that man ever stopped his hunting and gathering long enough to tell the rest of the world his story.

There are several rooms in the Lascaux caves, believed to have been aquifers, or deep wells, that were formed millions of years ago. Scientists believe that these rooms, upon their discovery by Paleolithic cavemen, served as refuge during storms, a storehouse for food and skins and weapons, and offered protection from wild animals. But they also became the cavemen's art studio. On the smooth walls the cavemen painted almost 1,500 works, possibly created over hundreds of years by several generations of residents. The earliest works of art on the cave walls are approximately 18,000 years old.

Most of the paintings are of large animals, primarily horses and stags, most in motion. But there are also felines, a bird, a bear, and a human. Dr. Randall Sword, who has been inside these caves, smelled the air, and touched the walls, believes that the raised or indented features of the walls' surface may have suggested the figures that ultimately appeared there. Although many images are painted with pigments from minerals, others have been incised upon the rock walls. The most famous of the stories hidden in the caves of Lascaux is told in a room called the Great Hall of the Bulls. Its several pictures describe *in a narrative* the discovery, the hunting, the capturing, and the killing of a herd of bison. The telling of the details of this particular day stretches across two huge walls deep within the recesses of the earth.

The art in the Lascaux caves represents the skill and precision of a succession of cave inhabitants over hundreds of years. But what stands out is that they had the time and will to create, and did it. There was very little in the way of language to communicate any details or design. There were no systems in place to create paint and brushes. Yet one or several of our forebears decided that they wanted to leave a mark on the world, and they did. And they left that mark in the form of a story, told on a wall.

It is astonishing to consider that these first known acts of human creativity were begun 12,000 years before the entombment of the pharaohs in the pyramids at Giza and 17,000 years before Michelangelo picked up a chisel for the first time. Yet they are connected. Each required the force of some individual's intellect to put these ideas into action.

The men and women who lived in the caves of Lascaux engaged their creative instinct to force out something new, something different, something never seen or known before. The art in these caves indicates on some level that it must be in our nature to create, to see the world in our own unique way, to share the significant details of our experience, and to be remembered for our great achievements. By creating, we both fulfill and live out our destiny, and preserve our stories so that those behind us can begin to understand what we have come to understand.

MICHELANGELO AND THE ANGEL

Michelangelo was one of the standout talents of the Italian Renaissance. Other than Leonardo da Vinci, he was without equal, then as now.

Michelangelo was a legendary creator. He was a painter, poet, sculptor, sketcher, cartoonist, author, and a student of the human form down to its deepest muscle and bone. One of his many creative challenges was to put into his art a semblance of the extraordinary images that must have been in his mind. His powers of visualization must have been remarkable as well, as there were no textbooks yet on the human form or its muscles and tendons and bones, yet he captured them so perfectly. He excelled in almost every art form, but his sculptures—particularly the *Pietà* in St. Peter's Basilica in Rome, the *David* in Florence, *The Captive Slaves* in the Louvre in Paris, and many others of his statuary, which adorn the world still—are considered to be some of the greatest ever created by man.

For some unknown reason, Michelangelo destroyed many of his sketches and drafts near the end of his life, but what has survived—of course, in addition to his many permanent works—is one explanation in his own words of how he came to sculpt some of the greatest works in the history of art. He did not write down many things about himself, but somehow a single quote of his survived hundreds of years, to the present day. It best describes how he managed his own creativity in his art and sculpture.

In response to a question about how he was able to convey such innocence on the face of one of his sculptures, he said, "I saw an angel in the rock and chipped around him, until he was free."

Michelangelo must have known himself very well to make such a statement, and further knew how his creativity was best encouraged. That he would let images "emerge" from the stone or canvas before him shows that he knew his efforts required great patience. And this is a concept that can be useful to any of us as we challenge ourselves, whether to create a book or screenplay, art or sculpture, a building or an ad campaign. Suppose that instead of forcing the issue when trying to create something, we let it emerge. Instead of demanding that the subject matter bend *to* our will, we let it *bend* our will. Instead of sculpting the marble of our intellect to make an image that is unnatural or overthought, imagine if we could be patient enough to chip around an idea that is already there. Instead of getting in the way of all of the angels in the marble, what would it be like if we could just set them free?

Michelangelo's creative process, at least as revealed in the quote, seemed to me to be strikingly similar to that of Alan Bergman. This kind of artistic process hinges on allowing your art to reveal itself to you. Though separated by four hundred years, and all the developments in life and living and technology that have come in between, both artistic processes hinge on allowing your art to reveal itself to you— which can happen only when we become confident in our vision. Bergman, Michelangelo, and countless artists in between have utilized and maximized their creative potential in very similar ways by using this method.

REMBRANDT PAINTED A LOT OF SELFIES

Rembrandt was a great artist, painter, sketcher, and visionary. He was able to capture emotion in his portraits unlike anyone before or since, and not only did he bring to the world a great body of work, he also exerted a powerful artistic influence on his generation and every generation of painters since.

After achieving many early career successes, Rembrandt made a number of bad personal and business decisions. First, he married a widow whose husband had been his business partner. This did not sit well with the morals of the time and place, namely Amsterdam in the 1600s. Not long after the marriage, they sold her house and moved into a much nicer neighborhood, far from where all the other painters lived. Painters at that time were craftsmen or artisans—like carpenters or potters or silversmiths. When Rembrandt moved uptown to live with his new wife in a distinctly upper-class neighborhood, he learned that all of his customers who lived there liked him as a painter but not as a neighbor. Many of them soon became former customers.

He and his young wife then began to face other enormous difficulties. They lost three children while trying to start a family. Then there was the matter of the large mortgage Rembrandt had taken out to buy the new house, which started to strangle him financially. But then he brought his career to very near a standstill. Hoist by his own petard, he brought his career to very near a standstill.

In those days, men in guilds or other groups hired a portraitist to memorialize their organization, either staged in a formal setting or captured in the throes of their exploits. Rembrandt was hired as a portraitist by the Company of Frans Cocq, a private militia. But instead of honoring the tradition of the times, Rembrandt chose to break the mold. In the painting *The Night Watch*, not only are the men portrayed just standing around and milling about, but Rembrandt apparently inserted *himself* into the painting as a bystander, looking over the shoulder of a man in a tall hat. He photobombed his most important work. The portrait was totally out of step with the spirit of the commission. Rembrandt might have misunderstood what they were after, or he simply ignored the chance to pay complete respect and bring deserved solemnity to the work. His patrons were particularly upset. It was seen as an act of insouciance and it cost his already damaged reputation significantly. He was in a perfect storm. Soon after the misunderstanding of *The Night Watch*, he found himself exhausted of goodwill and good patrons.

Unable to drum up enough business, Rembrandt was out of money, and soon drowning in debt. His wife, who had already lost three babies, died giving birth to their fourth child. He brought in a nanny, another widow, to take care of that son, and soon began a relationship with her. When that went sour, he undertook a romance with his maidservant. She got pregnant as well and he was required to provide her with support. And then, in a crescendo of disaster and very near bankruptcy, he transferred all his assets to his fifteen-year-old son so that the inheritance could be saved, but nonetheless he was forced to sell nearly all of his possessions because of his obligations to moneylenders.

But here is the most interesting aspect of his descent. No matter how bad things got, his life in tatters and ruins, Rembrandt never stopped creating. He worked on something every day, whether a sketch, an etching, or an oil painting. But with fewer and fewer customers, he could find fewer subjects to sit for him—no customers, no subjects. This is the reason why so many of his portraits later in his life are self-portraits. According to the Rembrandt House Museum, there are more than 150 self-portraits in his collection. He painted himself over and over, *because he had nothing else to paint*. What's more, many of these works of Rembrandt in various poses and states of dress were in layers and layers on the same canvases. These weren't portraits necessarily; they were his practice pads, just so he could keep his skills intact and his mind from slipping away.

One might say he was just keeping himself busy, giving himself something to do instead of thinking about all of his bad decisions. But just as likely, his painting was his refuge, and the only moments of free-dom he could find were when he was working. The regrets of his existence were lost in the magic of his art. Consider what he must have been dealing with on a day-to-day basis, with debts and court and financial obligations for money he did not have, yet he found hours and hours each day to devote to his painting.

Just one thing stood by him during all of the may-hem. One ally—his creativity—never departed when all others looked away. The self-portraits are the proof. They are the product of the creativity burning inside him, despite all that was going on around and outside him. With no outlet for his creativity, with all of his customers gone and his world crumbling, he satisfied his muse the only way he could. He looked in the mirror and kept on painting, kept on etching, kept on creating. For Rembrandt, his creativity was the one thing he could count on when other joys were long gone. It was his lifeline. He was keeping his cre-ative skills intact, and, in so doing, he was keeping his mind alert and alive. By forcing his intellect to continue being creative, no matter what else was going on in his life, he gave himself safe haven. Without continuing to exercise his creative instinct and pursue his intellectual muse, he would have had nothing, and must have known it somehow.

MOZART'S DESCRIPTION OF
HIS CREATIVE PROCESS

Mozart was one of the first child stars, the Michael Jackson of his day, the Justin Bieber of the 1700s. He was performing publicly, often on both the violin and keyboard, at age four. He was among the earliest musicians who tried unsuccessfully to break down the barriers that existed between art and commerce, between working for a pope or a prince and working for a living. In the end, he was never able to fully break through to achieve financial independence and to earn the living he deserved. In that era, long before royalties and copyrights, the great composer scrambled to earn a living at all, begging the question: How much more music would Mozart have lived to create if he had not had to create so much music just to live?

Mozart wrote some 650 pieces of musical art. In those days, after the first few performances, these remarkable pieces quickly lost any value. A musical instrument in the home was still somewhat of a luxury, and the music publishing business was in its infancy. The concert subscription model was the standard protocol for composers, but then, as now, only the very finest and most famous musicians could fill a concert hall full of wealthy types to hear a piece of music that had never been heard before. It did not allow many musicians to sustain a decent income, Mozart being one of them. Music as a career was based on a system of patronage, and "royalties" were usually what one called the king and queen.

Many of Mozart's greatest works were effectively valueless in the circles of society he was trying so hard to be part of, the same ones he kept getting kicked out of. He was recognized on the streets and in the palaces of many European cities, a century before there was even photography, but he could not make enough money to live well, and sustain a life for himself and his family. Genius was hardly recognized in those days, and genius without a decent income was a heartless way to live.

Many of Mozart's ideas on music, life, art, survival, and religion, among other topics, are captured in his writings—hundreds of letters to his sister and father and others. Insights into his creative process are scattered among the details of his everyday life in Salzburg and Vienna in these documents.

He was able to stand outside himself and look in, making perfect sense of what he was doing and what he was here for. In one letter, written when he was still in his teens, he was seemingly in awe of himself and his own ability. The following quote is from a letter to Friedrich Rochlitz, a German music critic who became one of Mozart's correspondents, summarizing Mozart's view of how he wrote. He said: "Writing, my subject enlarges itself, becomes methodized and defined, and the whole, though it be long, stands almost complete and finished in my mind, so that I can survey it, like a fine picture or a beautiful statue, at a glance." He is describing the sweet beauty of admiring that thing that *his mind* had just created, which he had known for only moments. He was able to both create and understand the nature of his creativity at the same time. All that was left for him to do was write it down—something he referred to as "tedious." He went on to say, in this same letter to Rochlitz: "In my imagination I do not hear the parts playing successively, I hear them *all at once* [my emphasis]. When I proceed to write down my ideas, they rarely differ from what they were in my imagination. A delight is all this inventing, this producing of music . . . it takes place as if in a pleasing, lively dream."

Creativity then was the same as it is now. That was only 250 years ago or so. . . . Man has not evolved all *that* much in evolutionary terms in that short period of time. It is not all that improbable to imagine that we can utilize our thinking the way Mozart did his. It is not impossible to believe that we can create like he did, or at least try. He was not the only composer who did it this way, either. According to Professor D. Kern Holoman, an expert on French composer Hector Berlioz, Berlioz would say, "I've finished my symphony, now all I have to do is write it down." Suppose you could try to adopt just this one aspect of their creative practices by allowing ideas to appear, uninhibited and unmolested, and then just transcribing them; making few, if any, changes in the first draft; skipping details if they are not ready yet; and making every effort to capture, in one piece, the results of the work your intellect has already completed.

You have to expect the possibility that a "whole idea" may enter your world . . . the whole song, the whole speech, the whole conversation you need to have, the whole play you are writing, the whole building you are designing. And you must let your imagination deliver this idea to you without any interruptions or harassment, enabling the best of your creativity, the purest of your efforts to emerge. By having faith in your intellect and its process, you can learn to trust the creativity that is happening, and capture it when it finally reveals itself.

Let yourself create like Mozart said he did, as if in a pleasing, lively dream.

BEETHOVEN COULD NOT PLAY THE VIOLIN

During his peak years, Beethoven was the best piano player in the world. He performed publicly for the first time at age seven. At thirteen he was paraded before Mozart to play Bach's Well-Tempered Clavier. In his teens he was the principal conductor and performer of his early piano concertos, and played them all over Europe to great response. He was a master composer as well, and enjoyed consistent success for his many subscription concerts introducing his new works. He lived his life as an outlier. He broke every rule he could find, both in his life and in his writing of music. He tore up the rule book for the way musicians earned their living and challenged the system of patronage then in place. When explaining why he would not live and work in the court and wear a uniform every day (like Franz Joseph Haydn and most others gladly did), Beethoven said to one monarch, "You are who you are because of your blood. I am who I am because I am Beethoven." He insisted that his talent should allow him to rise above the glass ceiling that kept composers on the same level as carpenters and other artisans in the class system of the time. Walking with the poet Goethe one day in the city of Teplitz, Beethoven refused to take off his hat in the presence of the empress and her court, and walked right through the courtiers without so much as a respectful nod. According to legend, his rudeness in this circumstance cost him his friendship with Goethe. He approached the outer boundaries of music in his later writings because he found that the conventions of tonal music did not allow him enough freedom to get his musical ideas across. In some passages of his later works, the *Grosse Fugue* string quartet, for instance, there are harbingers of atonal music, some ninety years before Arnold Schoenberg, Alban Berg, and Anton Webern formed their "school" of serial music.

But despite the facts of his impact on music and composition, Beethoven did not play many of the instruments he composed music for.

Admittedly, the principal instrument of Beethoven's life was the keyboard. But second only to his writing for that instrument was his writing for the violin. In most all of his compositions, there is a violin part. Almost all of the chamber music features it, whether violin sonatas, piano trios, or string quartets. In his one opera, *Fidelio*, the violin also carries a lot of freight. And of course the violin is the primary melodic vehicle in his nine symphonies and countless concerti. The violin was his "go-to" sound, the key to his creativity. Yet he could hardly play the instrument himself, even though it was such an important ally of his creative freedom and repertoire.

The first evidence of his even studying the violin with any serious intent indicates that he was twenty-two years old, ancient by string player standards. Just a few years later, at age thirty-one, he began to lose his hearing, and since it is practically impossible to play the violin in tune without excellent hearing, he certainly never would have played much after that. When he wrote his one and only violin concerto, Violin Concerto in D Major, he needed his close friend and one of the best violinists of the day, Ignaz Schuppanzigh, to show him the upper reaches of the instrument and confirm that a violinist could play the part as Beethoven had written it. Why? Because Beethoven could not play those parts himself. This conclusion, however controversial, is based on facts as detailed in a letter I received from Patricia Stroh, curator of the Beethoven Center at San Jose State University in

California. I had asked her if it was true that the great composer was a poor violinist. She wrote: "What is known about Beethoven's violin playing later in life comes primarily from the reminiscences of Ferdinand Ries (Beethoven's pupil, whose father gave Beethoven violin lessons in Bonn) and Gerhard von Breuning (whose father was a violinist and heard Beethoven's violin playing). Ries's description of Beethoven's violin playing as an adult is in Franz Wegeler's *Biographische Notizen über Ludwig van Beethoven.*[1] Beethoven and Ries played some of Beethoven's violin sonatas together, with Beethoven at the violin; Ries described this as 'truly dreadful music-making, because in the throes of his enthusiasm he did not hear when he attacked a passage with the wrong fingering.' There is also a brief discussion of Beethoven's violin playing in the book *Beethoven: Violin Concerto* by Robin Stowell.[2]

In Vienna, Beethoven received some violin lessons from Wenzel Krumpholz and Ignaz Schuppanzigh but "evidently made little progress." In his reminiscences, Gerhard von Breuning relates what his father

---

[1] F. Wegeler. Translated into English as *Beethoven Remembered: The Biographical Notes of Franz Wegeler and Ferdinand Ries* (Arlington, VA: Great Ocean Publishers, 1987), 106.

[2] R. Stowell. *Beethoven: Violin Concerto* (Cambridge: Cambridge University Press, 1998), 2–3.

told him, namely that Beethoven "never had any particular purity of tone on the fiddle nor any outstanding ability on it; he was always likely to play out of tune even before his hearing was affected; thereafter, of course, his playing was increasingly out of tune until deafness made him give it up completely."[3]

But his inability to play the violin well did not in any way inhibit his ability to write for the violin. The fact that he was not a master of the instrument did not prevent him from creating some of the great masterpieces of that instrument's repertoire, bringing about theretofore unknown nuances in its sound, its capabilities, its place in the orchestra, and its voice in popular culture.

This illustrates one of the great freedoms that creativity allows, namely that one does not have to *do* something particularly well in order to *create* for that thing. Creativity is a limitless function of your intellect that allows you to see, hear, and imagine empty spaces filled with sounds or images that are not there, at least not yet, whether music, words, art, buildings, or anything else your mind can imagine, irrespective of the level of ability you may possess in a particular area. My father, Preston Sturges, is considered one of

[3] G. von Breuning, ed. M. Solomon. *Memories of Beethoven* (Cambridge: Cambridge University Press, 1992), 28–29.

the great filmmakers. He was the first screenwriter to direct his own script and won the first Academy Award for Best Original Screenplay. Despite his ability to write for other actors, and tell them exactly how to say each line perfectly and hilariously, he himself could not act at all. He never performed as an actor in any of his movies and was never invited by anyone else to do so in any other movies, either, at least during his heyday, despite his great celebrity at the time.

Earlier I mentioned several other fields that welcome creators who imagine and realize amazing things but cannot themselves actually participate in the ultimate result, simply because they lack the ability. Fashion designers illustrate this point on a yearly basis on the runways of Paris and during New York's Fashion Week. Architects, even the best ones, are rarely the builders of the buildings and houses they imagine. In her book on creativity, *The Creative Habit*, Twyla Tharpe makes the argument that creativity requires expertise, practice, and dedication, which in some cases is true, but not in *all* cases. Expertise is a significant factor but not if it serves only as a limitation.

Beethoven could not play the violin very well, and so what?

IRVING BERLIN AND HIS
FAMOUS CRANK

Irving Berlin was the great early twentieth-century American songwriter who composed such iconic works as "God Bless America," "White Christmas," "Puttin' on the Ritz," "I'll Be Seeing You," and "Cheek to Cheek." Without his contributions, the Great American Songbook would be missing many pages.

But as great a songwriter as he was, he was a very limited piano player. In describing his ability, he once went so far as to call it modest, and even that may have been an exaggeration. But he devised a shortcut to circumvent his lack of ability and allow his creativity to burst forth from him despite being unable to play the instrument that enabled that very same creativity to exist. What did he do? He learned how to play the piano and never hit any wrong notes. How, you ask? He played only the black keys!

If you play only the black keys, there are no wrong notes. Any two black keys you play sound good together. Any three black keys you play sound like a chord. And you can easily pound away for several minutes before arousing the suspicions of those around you that you are not really all that good and that you are just making some organized noise.

But the problem Berlin's solution created was that all of his songs were written in the same key, giving them a certain sameness. And since men and women often do not sing in the same key, he needed to be able to change keys and accommodate the different voices. So he had a special one-of-a-kind piano built for him that looked like a real piano in every respect except for the huge crank on its side. This crank actually changed the key of the whole piano, giving Berlin the freedom to write in another key or move up or down however many notes he needed while still only playing the black keys. Considering all the trouble he had to go through, it probably would have been just as easy to take a few piano lessons, but songwriters are a superstitious bunch, and once he began to succeed as a writer he did nothing at all to change his luck.

The wisdom of his experience is very clear: you must never let technology get in the way of your creativity. Even when the technology is the instrument you need to create on, just find a way. Figure out how to get around whatever technical complexity is keeping you from designing, painting, composing, or whatever it is you're trying to do. Berlin had to invent a new kind of piano in order to turn his creativity loose. What will you have to invent to turn yours loose? Just because something has not been thought of before does not mean it cannot be thought of now. There is a solution to every problem and there is no reason to dwell on the difficulties when you can just as easily think of the solutions. Solutions exist, possibly there just beyond your view, just out of reach, just around the corner. If you allow your imagination and creativity to work for you, your creative horizon is absolutely unlimited by any technological hurdle you may encounter.

One of the most successful songwriters in history was not a great piano player, yet he managed to change the world with his songs and music—and a crank.

ALBERT EINSTEIN ON GROOMING AND CREATIVITY

Albert Einstein said that he got all of his best ideas while shaving.

This quote speaks to the significance of the distracted mind in the creative process, a point illustrated also by both Mozart and Beethoven, who loved to take long walks as a way of inspiring themselves.

Einstein not only recognized the potential impact of his creations, most notably the secret of the universe, but that he also knew *when* his ideas would come to him shows an uncanny mastery of his own creative process.

We mortals, left to survey the products of the creative lives that came before us, can only hope to feel the same inspirations, somehow, someday. But if we know *when* our new ideas might arrive, we might be better prepared to utilize them when they do.

Enjoy your next shave, or other distraction, all the more.

PICASSO HAD NO CHOICE

Picasso had a different take on his creativity. He said that, unlike his contemporary Albert Einstein, he actually *never* knew when he would be inspired or even what would inspire him. He spent long days in his studio so that he would be ready to react when inspiration ultimately did strike. He said, "Inspiration exists, but it has to find you working." He wrote repeatedly that his art was his everything, and the pursuit of its existence was why he worked at it every day of his life. Without creating every day, whether a painting, a sculpture, a print, or a drawing, there was something missing. As he grew older, his work schedule actually increased, buoyed by his long-held superstition that only hard work would keep him alive. He believed that he had no choice—it was paint or die.

Proof of his devotion to his art can be found in this definitive statement he made about himself: "We artists are indestructible. Even in a prison, or a concentration camp, I would be almighty in my own world of art, even if I had to paint my pictures with my wet tongue on the dusty floor of my cell."

[Renoir actually lived this sad scenario. His arthritis gnarled his hands so badly at the end of his life that he could no longer even hold his brushes. An assistant would have to tie the brushes to Renoir's hands just so that he could keep painting!]

We cannot even begin to imagine the passion that swept through his heart every day. He must have known that he was the only one who could create these great works and that he was the only one who could ever truly understand what it was he was chasing after. He despised the opinions of others, especially traditionalists, and often said that good taste was the enemy of creativity.

We cannot be, any of us, Picasso. That story is one and done and will be told forever in the thousands of everlasting images created by him. But we can try to be like him. We can consider the possibility of being as passionate and devoted and committed to our creativity, even in some small way, as he was to his.

ALAN GREENSPAN USES A LITTLE BLACK BOX

I met Alan Greenspan at the Aspen Ideas Festival. He was there to discuss the future of the financial world, and I was there to present the book I was writing on creativity, which you now are reading. The fact is that he is a most creative man. His approach to his art—the art of finance—is uniquely creative and illuminates another way to utilize the passive intellect in the development of new ideas.

Greenspan reeks of genius, like good cologne. His immense capacity for thought and incredible intellectual fomentation are hard to hide. This is the man who basically ran the United States' and the world's economy for almost thirty years—through several administrations and numerous crises of confidence.

He witnessed the emergence of new nations and currencies; the birth and growth of several new technologies, including the Internet; watched the country get in and out of several wars; and all the while tried to make sure that everyone who was earning a living had a chance to establish and maximize their wealth.

I asked him if he believed there was much room for creativity in his line of work. He nodded emphatically. He explained that very few people knew that he had been a clarinet player in jazz bands for many years. In high school he played with Stan Getz before attending the Juilliard School and was sufficiently proficient upon graduation to join Woody Herman's band, the Thundering Herd. I asked him how creativity finds a place in his life and work now, all these years later. He crossed his arms in front of him, looked at me funny, and said this: "I have a little black box. [He tapped his head at the temple—indicating where the box was kept.] And when I have problem I need to solve, I put everything I know about that problem inside the little black box. Every scrap, every detail. Then I close the box. I go for a swim or take a walk. Later, when I open the box and look inside, the answer is usually very clear to me."

As Greenspan was talking I realized what he was saying and understood the process he was actually describing: He completely trusts his intellect to provide the solutions to his most difficult problems. He gives his mind and brain all the information that is available and then gets away from it and lets his intellect take care of the rest. He trusts himself. He trusts his thinking. He trusts his process. All he needs to do is see clearly the solution his mind is providing, and act on it, or not, depending on what is best for that particular situation. Faced with complex decisions that have many implications and myriad possibilities, he lets the supercomputer between his ears do the analysis, the spreadsheets, the PowerPoints, the heavy lifting, leaving him, at the end of the day, with the simple decision of a yes or a no.

There is an incredible power and practically unlimited freedom that comes with trusting your intellect to simply finish the assignment to which it has been assigned. The results will be individual to you—and thus unique, artistic, and creative—as you give in to the thoughts that have never been thought before. Oh yeah, and don't forget to get yourself a little black box.

Ten Things You Can Do with a . . .

❖❖❖

This intellectual exercise has been around for quite a few years and was recently referenced in Malcolm Gladwell's book *Outliers*. Gladwell describes a test given to students in the UK that was intended to measure the outer reaches of their imaginations. The answers provided an unexpected and extraordinary view of each subject's intellectual reach.

But all I saw in it was a great creative exercise. This is a test of imagination without limits. First the subject can be a brick, the next time a paintbrush, and then a hot air balloon, and so on until there are no more things with which to do ten things.

At some point Steve Jobs asked himself the question, "What are ten things we can do with a cell phone?" His answers changed the world. He set his mind free and began to realize that the phone could actually be almost anything. Thanks to him using this very same exercise, your cell phone is now a computer, a still and video camera, an Internet search engine, a way to read books and watch movies, an app warehouse, a downloading device, a writing tool and note taker, a game center, a music composition device, a drum machine, a music storage center, and, of course, it's a telephone. Let him be your inspiration.

Ask yourself, what are ten things you can do with . . . A walking stick. A long piece of pipe. Three feet of strong rope. A broken golf club. A ballpeen hammer. An unfinished poem. Four hundred dollars. A roomful of smart kids. A day alone in Hong Kong. A tuning fork. Two old tennis racquets. A piano. Six hundred pieces of recycled paper. A sailboat at anchor. An outright lie. Or anything else you can imagine.

Creativity is a force within us that bursts out—imagining things that are not there, yet. Let yours fly, regardless of how much sense the answers make or don't make. Write them all down somewhere and keep the ideas safely tucked away, not only as a measure of what your intellect is capable of seeking, but as an idea trove to which you can return when you need it.

CREATIVITY AND
THE BRAIN

SOME FACTS ABOUT THE BRAIN

Mark Tramo is uniquely suited to understand the brain and the creative process. He studied theater and music while an undergraduate at Yale, and then went to medical school at Cornell. He got his PhD in neurobiology at Harvard. He has been published in *Science* and the *Journal of Neurophysiology*. I attended one of his lectures at UCLA; we spoke at length afterward. I wanted to spend a minute with someone who knew so much about my brain. He was still awestruck in a childlike way by the brain's capacity to process ideas and create new ones on a constant and regular basis.

He was kind enough to let me ask every question I could think of regarding the brain, how it works and fails, how it creates, and so forth. His answers gave me, a nonscientist and technically challenged neophyte, many insights into the brain and how it works. Some of the questions: What is the difference between a creative thought and an emotional thought in scientific terms? From a physiological perspective, are creative people's brains different from everyone else's? To the brain and its cognitive functions, is there a difference between thinking about art and thinking about science? Does the brain know it is "creating"? What happens to the brain when we dream, daydream, or simply "feel" creative? His reply? "All good questions. But we don't really know all the answers yet."

Tramo acknowledged that until very recently—within the past twenty years or so—precious little was known about the creative part of the brain and how it works, considering how much time and effort had been devoted to understanding exactly those facts. The brain is only now beginning to give up some of its incredible secrets. But how the brain works when an idea is created or how it manages to hold on to ideas that have been created are just two of many functions of the brain that are still not fully understood. Tramo said that there are "conventions of thought" or "understandings" of what *should* be happening in our brains, but still, it's too early to paint a coherent picture of what a brain that's creating looks like. What seems clear is that the frontal lobes are important to creativity and that perhaps "less is more." In other words, in order for creativity to take place, somehow we shut down some parts of the brain while we activate others. But much goes on at the cellular level and in the chemistry and micro-circuitry of the human brain about which nobody has a clue. There is a "void" in the science.

So while there is still so much that we do not know, here are some things Tramo was able to share about the brain, the instrument of our creativity.

First of all, the brain weighs only about three pounds. Spread out evenly on a flat surface, like a homolographic projection of the earth, the entire cerebral cortex would be about the size of a hubcap, a quarter of an inch thick.

Second, there are more than one hundred billion neurons in the brain, and more than one hundred trillion synapses. Every sensation, feeling, thought, and memory we know is the result of signals that are passed between neurons via synapses. A simple idea might take hundreds of millions of neurons and synapses and the connections between them in order to be created.

Third, neurons "splash" or "spray" each other across synapses with both excitatory *and* inhibitory substances during the process of thought. These cause a bloom of readiness in "connected" neurons and synapses in the brain, which in turn allows ideas to travel among the network, at speeds believed to be about twenty-five miles per hour. This measurement is called "conduction velocity."

Fourth, as a result of all the thinking and the connecting and the spraying, the brain needs to dispose of the wastes that its thoughts and thinking processes have produced. It is for this reason that the brain has a sewer. What ends up in the sewer becomes part of our spinal fluid.

Fifth, if you took every neuron soma (that is, a cell body) in a human brain, all one hundred billion plus or so, and laid them end to end in a long straight line, a single brain would stretch about nine hundred miles, or roughly the distance from Los Angeles to Aspen, Colorado.

Sixth, when your eyes see an image of something shocking or painful, someone getting stuck with a pin, for instance, a part of your brain reacts to that image and it is the same part of your brain that would react if *you* had been stuck with the pin. The neurons in this part of the brain are called "mirror neurons." Mirroring plays an important role in how we learn communication skills, as well as empathy and creativity.

Last, and certainly not least, is this most extraordinary fact about our brains: The entirety of that portion of the brain that is the essence of our unique humanity—our memories, our logic, our moral compass, our sense memory, our uniqueness, our yesterdays—all of it, of course including our greatest gift, our creativity, would fit into a space about the size of two coffee cups. That's right, just two! The differences between you and creative geniuses like Steve Jobs and Picasso are not so great when you consider that the most important and vital parts of their brains and yours could fit equally well into two Venti containers down at the local Starbucks.

We basically are our thoughts, and without fresh new ideas coming into existence, we are risking the chance of never knowing the joy of unadulterated creativity and the revitalization it provides. The brain is a remarkable instrument, yes, but only if we use it. It is at our service, waiting to be relied upon, challenged, and otherwise inspired to act for and on our behalf. The biological gifts evolution has handed us are nurtured by creativity. Take away our intellectual capacity and we are simply going through the motions of life and living. But enlivened and enriched with creativity, the brain can function and life can begin again, every day. Many neuroscientists, including Mark Tramo, believe that exercising the brain through forceful mental activities, such as creativity, is good for us in the short and long run.

SAVANTS AND PRODIGIES

The brain and mind are capable of incredible achievements, at any age and at almost any stage of physical development. Proof of this is the existence of prodigies. Prodigies are examples of what the mind can do in its purest and most unblemished state of being. Their genius displays itself before even their true human nature shows up. Their intellectual capacity is operating on a level they cannot even begin to understand.

One of the great musical prodigies ever has gone on to become one of the great violinists of this generation, Itzhak Perlman. He was a concertizing musician at age eight, and as is the tradition of that unique colony of artists, he almost always plays from memory. Every one of the many pieces he has learned contains thousands and thousands of notes. Not only does he remember every note he has to play, but also the composer's instructions for the tempo, key, rhythm, and, some say most important, the phrasing and nuance. He readily acknowledges that he has memorized hundreds of works since his childhood and can sit and play one or several of them for hours and hours in front of thousands of people. His mind is adorned with these millions of bits of information, stored forever, routinely and repeatedly accessed, and almost never mistaken for any other such bits of information. How is it even possible that there is that much room, so well organized and accessible, all in one man's head? And it has been that way since he was a child. Think for a moment about the amount of musical information he has stored, and the infinite room that exists for even more to *be* stored. It is an example of the capacity of the mind and what it is capable of accomplishing when pressed to do so. Is it creative? No, not really. But Perlman's ability to memorize, store, and access millions of facts of musical data illustrates the near-infinite amount of information the human brain is capable of learning and retaining.

Perlman said once, in a postconcert interview I

attended, that sometimes during a concert *his mind will wander.* While playing these hundreds of thousands of notes from memory in front of thousands of people, night after night, he will wonder where the car is parked or what city he is in. Unbelievable, no? His brain is literally flying through millions of commands and memories, musical notes and interpretations of their performance, yet it has the capacity to consider mundane questions about his location or transportation while doing so.

The brain's ability to retain information is also illustrated by savants. People with savant syndrome often have mental disorders coupled with an over-achieving ability to learn and memorize, though usually in a very narrow range of knowledge. Savants present a portrait of the efficiency of the brain, but in their case it is usually only one part of the brain that works remarkably well, while many other functions are impaired or even inoperable. One of the most well-known savants was Kim Peek, who developed a depth of knowledge so deep that he could recall practically *everything* he ever read or saw. Yes, ever. He was the inspiration for Dustin Hoffman's character in the film *Rain Man.* Peek would open a book and read both facing pages at the same time—each with one eye. This allowed him to read thousands of books during his lifetime. He could retain and recall practically every detail. No matter how many years prior the knowledge was acquired, it stayed with him. He could remember the day of the week of an important historical event, and often what the weather was like, too. He also learned the language of music and would read piano sonatas and symphonic scores. Near the end of his life, according to his father, because he remembered everything he read, he would correct actors if they got words wrong in a performance of a play. "That's not what it says in the book," he would shout. Like many savants, he was gifted in that one area but completely lost when he strayed from his unique path of genius. He could not rhyme or make puns. Metaphors would anger him because he was not capable of empirical thought, and a metaphor was not a fact. His social interactions were awkward and he often left off speaking in midsentence. He could not dress himself. He never learned to drive. His father had to accompany him everywhere because he had so little physical coordination. But what a mind, what an incredible mind, trapped in a body that could not make sense of the simplest tasks. He could not push a button through a buttonhole, but he could recite a Shakespeare soliloquy that he had read only once long before. His damaged brain gave him a prodigious capacity for recall.

What if the remarkable powers demonstrated by Kim Peek and Itzhak Perlman's intellects—the retention of facts, the capacity for memorization, the volume of knowledge at their fingertips, the strength of instant and immediate recall, the ability to never lose an acquired thought—could be turned into forces of creativity? In other words, suppose we could use more and more of our intellectual prowess as part of our creative process. That might change everything.

I bring up these two examples of the brain's capacity to illustrate, at least on one level, the capability we all possess. The brain can be a remarkable partner, if we let it be.

THE BRAIN AS A BODY OF WATER — AN IMAGINING

As one way of looking at the human brain, imagine for a moment that it is a beautiful and pristine lake, untouched and unblemished, so clear that you can practically see to the bottom.

In this imagining, a new thought can come from anywhere. It might be like a gust of wind blowing across the surface, the disturbance causing hundreds of thousands of ripples. For us, this is not unlike hearing a great speaker discuss a great idea, and just like that, hundreds of thousands of synapses fire in response, creating a unique sequence with every new idea that occurs.

Or an idea can bubble up from deep below, somewhere in the darkness, created by some long-lost inspiration forgotten for years but now hurtling to the surface. It might have been loosened by the equivalent of an underwater earthquake. When this happens to us, we often call these aha moments. Or we call them epiphanies and base the remainder of our lives on the logic created by the upsurge of those thoughts.

Memory in this daydream is a huge field of unfriendly seaweed, moving in slow motion across the water, ensnaring everything that it touches. But because it is always moving, things are never necessarily where they are supposed to be. And this is why we cannot find the words we need, cannot remember someone's name, or cannot recall a long-remembered poem we swore never to forget.

Cognizance and instinct are like schools of fish or pods of whales that travel anywhere they want, anytime they want, creating a poignant and potent force deep within the intellect, influencing every thought they encounter.

Creativity is the freedom that comes with believing that there is no perimeter, that there is no stopping, that the possibilities of thought are endless. It is the power to believe that there is no shoreline. Creativity is having faith in the sanctity and perfection of an unlimited imagination and the joy of knowing that ideas are infinitely available, always being refreshed by some deep underground stream feeding into the pristine lake.

THE HARMONICS OF THINKING

When a stringed instrument is plucked or bowed and generates sound, the noise includes several other sounds as well, including vibrations, reverberations, overtones, partials, and waves. Some we hear, some we cannot hear. The sound is actually a blend of many vibration frequencies that resonate with one another. Strum the open strings on a guitar, for instance, and let the notes ring, and you will hear notes plus their harmonics echoing. Play a chord on a piano and hold the sustain pedal down and you will hear a number of sounds as other strings join in. The strings of the chord you are playing are vibrating, causing other strings of the instrument to vibrate sympathetically as the harmonics are triggered and engaged.

The creative intellect similarly gives off harmonics: the harmonics of thinking. A new idea is not just an isolated intellectual event. It is part of an enormous process where neurons fire, excitatory sprays mist, synapses transmit, and millions or billions more neurons mist and synapses tingle at the prospect that they, too, might get in on the action. Once this phenomenon is under way, practically anything can happen. Ideas can begin anywhere and everywhere. One can lead to another and to another and to another. Idea harmonics echo throughout the intellect, finding sympathetic vibrations and reverberations in other places in your mind. That's what the synapses are for, to connect the neurons and the thoughts they are having. And just as on a piano, where untouched strings will start to vibrate in sympathy with strings that are being played, the "sound" of ideas in your intellect can inspire harmonics and other sympathetic vibrations in another part of your intellect as well.

The sound of one remarkable idea echoing and harmonizing is your creativity coming to life. Ideas will inspire other ideas, as a musical note inspires the harmonics of other notes. You may be searching for a solution to an architectural conundrum when suddenly a solution to a completely different problem will spring into place, brought to you as the "harmonic product" of the first idea.

A difficult experience may also create a whole set of idea harmonics. A seeming failure might be the action that plucks an intellectual string and sets off a whole sequence of new, more successful ideas. Walter Isaacson's biography on Steve Jobs describes Jobs being furiously inspired to act and think and create once he was removed and then returned as head of the fledgling and as yet unsuccessful Apple Inc. By the time he ran the company for the second time, years later, his head was bursting with new ideas and ways to implement them. Necessity, in this case a grand defeat that needed to be avenged, was the "sound" that encouraged his ideas to ring out and trigger harmonics and sympathetic vibrations in other places in his intellect.

And Steve Jobs did not just think differently about computers. The harmonics of his thoughts allowed him to think differently about *everything he saw and touched*, and it is a different world we live in as a result.

There is nothing off topic when it comes to thinking, and especially when it comes to creative thinking. Ideas can come from anywhere at any time, with or without any connection whatsoever to any other thoughts you might be having. The phenomenon of the creative intellect is that it is a constantly active panorama, with a 360-degree view.

So embrace your ideas *and* the harmonics of your ideas. They may be joined at the hip or they may be completely random, un-sequenced, non sequitur gems. One good thought can cause a sympathetic vibration of other thoughts, in other parts of your brain. Simply because it is not in step with other thoughts you might be having does not mean an idea is not workable or even remarkable. Sketch, scratch, preserve, capture *every* idea, and later on let it find its proper place.

Creativity is the ability to think of thoughts that have never been thought before and in ways that have not been thought before. This harmonics-of-thinking concept is an encouragement to you to be open and available to every idea that may appear on your creative horizon.

Reductions and More Reductions

❖❖❖

This exercise encourages you to simplify a story over and over, forcing your intellect to occupy smaller and smaller spaces each time. This is the basis of good writing according to E. B. White, the famed author of *Stuart Little* and *Charlotte's Web*, who wrote in his manual of writing, *The Elements of Style*, that "Rule 17 of the Principles of Composition is to Omit Needless Words." This is really just an exercise in omitting needless words.

Often, creativity is storytelling of one kind or another. Haiku, the traditional Japanese folk poetry, limits the creator to seventeen syllables in three lines in which to express his or her full creative mien and tell an entire tale. The stories on the walls of the caves of Lascaux, on the other hand, are practically limitless, telling more than fifteen hundred stories of early hunters and their prey.

Finding a different way to tell the same story is an exercise in creativity. This Reductions and More Reductions exercise requires that a story be told five different ways, each shorter and more to the point than the previous one.

PART ONE

Tell the Story in a Paragraph. Find a story that is familiar: *Romeo and Juliet*, *King Lear*, the tattered romance of Marilyn Monroe and Joe DiMaggio, a recent hit film, a current news item or a natural disaster—whatever strikes you. Tell the story in some detail, but no longer than a paragraph.

PART TWO

Turn the Paragraph into a Sentence. Take the same story, and now reduce it. However long and complex the story was as a paragraph, now turn that story into a single sentence. Use only the most significant highlights to make this step work successfully.

PART THREE

Turn the Sentence into a Headline. Reduce the entire story yet again, now into a *New York Times*–style headline of no more than four or five words. This further simplification forces you to be even more concise than before, using fewer words to say just as much while still retaining the shape and essence of the story.

PART FOUR

Turn the Headline into a Single Word. This is the penultimate step of this exercise. Simplify the story even further, now just to its basic intent, but in only one word. This is similar to what authors and book publishers will do. They often use a single word to tell a story and title a book, such as *Blink, Heidi, Shōgun, Dracula, M.A.S.H.,* and *Steppenwolf,* to name just a few. (Clearly my publisher and I ignored this guideline.) One-word titles appear in film and theatrical pieces as well, including *Pygmalion, Arthur, Bambi, Frozen, 10, Help, Wicked, Ratatouille,* and many others. For the exercise, search for the one word that tells the story best.

PART FIVE

Turn the Headline into an Onomatopoeia. Literally these are words that just make a sound, words that make the sound of what they are. Usually they are not verbs or nouns, simply phonetic representations of noise. Used very successfully in comic books and political cartoons, well-known onomatopoeias include "pow," "crunch," "splat," "zoink," "kablam," "kablooie," and "hmmm." This final step reduces the story to its emotional gristle.

The Reductions and More Reductions exercise ultimately tells the same story five different ways, with each iteration still capturing the dramatic arc and essence of the story, but with fewer and fewer words each time, until there are none.

CREATIVITY AND YOU: TWELVE IDEAS TO MAXIMIZE YOUR CREATIVE POTENTIAL

IN ORDER FOR ANYONE—WHETHER YOU ARE A writer, a poet, a student, an executive, a lawyer, a chef, or an architect—to understand how creativity can play a continuing and vital role in your life, you must be able to guide and manage your own creative process.

While that process is uniquely different for each individual creator, there are many elements of creativity that are the same for everyone who succeeds at it. For instance, you have to be devoted. You have to be passionate about your art. You have to be unafraid.

All givens, really. Without devotion, passion, and fearlessness, there is no foundation for creativity.

But there are less obvious pitfalls and roadblocks that can prevent creativity from finding its proper momentum. There are mistakes we all make that reduce the effectiveness of our creative efforts. Without meaning to, we even diminish the quality of the time we are able to give to it with needless and unnecessary distractions.

The development of a successful creative process requires you to get rid of anything that prevents creativity from reaching its full potential. The introduction and implementation of the right guidelines can allow you this freedom, and do wonders for you and your creativity. These are largely uncomplicated fixes and simple changes to make. Most are inspired by or taken from my conversation notes of literally thousands of meetings and listening sessions with hundreds of writers, producers, artists, and executives.

KEEP YOUR PROCESS TO YOURSELF

Creativity is an uncertain gift. It can be unwieldy. It can be elusive. To try to get in touch with it in the first place is hard enough, much less to rediscover it, again and again.

Neil Young's manager, Elliot Roberts, told me that Neil says he approaches every new song like it's a wild animal in a cage; that he sneaks up on it, trying not to disturb it, as it reveals itself to him. He has that much respect for his own process. I take from this that he is never complacent about it, and that he treasures every individual opportunity and inspiration. And this is one of the great rock songwriters. His statement reveals that his process, as it should be, is a very private thing, known only to him.

Each individual creator identifies for him- or herself a different way to get it done. As you learn how to find a place for creativity in your life, I believe you must absolutely keep it to yourself. The how and why of your creative success is nobody's business but your own. The less light that shines on it, the longer it will last, the longer it will continue to work for you. None of the top writers that I have worked with ever discuss it. Ever. They have too much respect for it to talk about it.

The only writers I have met who freely analyze their creative process are the rookies, those who don't even know that they should never do that. One of the reasons why the music business has so many one-hit wonders is because the individuals did not realize how they wrote that hit, and thus they were never able to identify and repeat the steps that brought all that success to their door. But you can be sure they told anyone who was willing to listen that it took only twenty minutes, came to them in a dream, was the easiest money they ever made, etc. Arrogance is no friend of the creative process.

Allow yourself the joy of your creativity, but also allow yourself the freedom to keep the process a private matter. There is no need to show off to the world, to tell everyone how you mastered your latest masterpiece. Treat the gift of your creativity like a precious priceless crystal you found one day out in the world. Be in awe of it. Enjoy its place in your life like a great love. Its mystery is its magic. Pursue its great potential, but show that you respect it too much to talk about it behind its back.

Just create. Be thankful that creativity exists in your life and move on from there. When you have an idea, capture it. When you find a solution, remember it. When an idea pops out of the oven, tiptoe over to a desk and sketch it before it disappears. Tell no one what your process enables you to do. You will be challenging only your own creativity, whatever it is and however it feeds itself. As with all good secrets, the less said about it the better.

PRACTICE CREATIVITY BY VISUALIZING

One form of creativity is visualization, and by that I mean the ability to see things that are not there. This kind of creativity is your imagination doing what comes most naturally: seeing or hearing possibilities not yet in place, spheres not yet in motion. Cities, buildings, melodies, plays, medical breakthroughs, all manner of inventions . . . all started as nothing! Each was, at some point, just a thought that had never been thought before. Everything was just an idea, once upon a time, being visualized by its creator.

Visualizing is like daydreaming, just more organized, more forcefully inspired. It is the practice of imagining things that have never been things before, willfully picturing new ideas, creating new solutions, dreaming new dreams.

According to Mark Tramo, the brain already has the ability to bring the future into the present. It anticipates what is about to take place, as a way of protecting us from danger, and apparently does this without us doing anything. It is a built-in feature of the machine that is the brain. He says that visualizing future as present is the product of millions of years of evolution. It is our genetic gift and provides us the distinct evolutionary advantage we enjoy now on a daily basis.

So why not take better advantage of this gift? Use it to practice your creativity. Encourage yourself and your creative mind to see and hear and smell and taste the world not just for what it is but for what it could be, for what it can be, what it might be. Actively practice visualizing things that are not there yet.

For instance, look thirty seconds into the future and see what will take place . . . in a restaurant, at an intersection, watching a film, reading a book. Try to imagine a friendship where there are just two people sitting at a bus stop. Hear what they might say to each other. Try to see where a baseball diamond would fit in an abandoned and vacant inner-city block where there are now just used mattresses with tires and litter strewn about.

Practice your visualization by setting your imagination free at every opportunity. It might look like you're talking to yourself sometimes, but so what?

Visualizing what is not yet here, hearing what is not yet sound, tasting what is not yet a recipe, and so forth: these are all the creative imagination at play. The more comfortable you can be at practiced visualizing, the more you will enable your gift to flourish.

FINISH WHAT YOU START

Creativity commences simply enough, usually with a spark, a flash, a "wow" moment. You race to grab a pen and something to write on, and capture as much of it as you can remember. But often what the idea really needs is not a beginning but an ending.

When a creative thought begins, we know there is a rippling of millions of synapses firing in a sequence never fired before, followed by the joy and shiver of a pure thought being birthed, followed by the "aaaaah" of some kind of epiphany. This can happen at any time, whether you are expecting it or not. It is an involuntary act to think, so how your creativity begins is completely uncontrollable. But how that thought gets completed is entirely up to the person doing the thinking.

As a standard practice of your creativity, once an idea hits you, finish *some* version of it. One writer I knew was very comfortable writing the first verse and chorus of songs. He would call me and say, let me play you something. He would proudly sing the unfinished work, and ask what I thought. My question was always the same: Where's the rest of it? He was too quick to seek approval and recognition. By the time he went back to try to write the second verse, the bridge, the outro, and so forth, there was nothing there. His mind had moved on. The singular vision required to complete the thought had changed its focus and was gone, likely forever. Needless to say I never gave him a deal. Remember how Gerry Goffin would deal with this same dilemma? Like a professional. He wouldn't begin until he knew where he needed to end. He was patient, and, like Mozart, allowed the entire idea to reveal itself to him before committing it to paper. Which is just one reason why he is in the Songwriters Hall of Fame and deserves all the credit he gets.

Only you can complete your thought, whatever it is. Before you get up and walk away, make sure it has a beginning and an ending. Do not to let your idea just sit there unfinished. You may never have the chance again, and certainly you will never be in that particular frame of mind again.

By finishing a first draft, this finalizes things in the mind, names the file in which it will reside, and completes the circle of thought. When you return to further develop the idea, hours or days or weeks later, you will find that all of the basic components are outlined for you, left neat and tidy and ready for further attention.

TAKE FULL ADVANTAGE OF
THE GOLDEN HOUR

In the tragedy of war, if you can treat an injured person within the first hour of their sustaining the injury, the chances of their ultimate recovery are much higher. These first sixty minutes will determine the quality of the rest of that person's life and are referred to as the "golden hour."

In creativity, there is a golden hour. It starts with those first precious moments right after a new idea has just revealed itself, right after the bloom of inspiration has suddenly appeared. Whatever the idea ultimately is or finally becomes, how you treat it in its first few minutes, in the golden hour, determines its fate.

New ideas do not come with name tags or road signs or elaborate orchestral cues. They show up, often suddenly and out of nowhere, and it is up to you to notice them. It is up to you to make sure they do not disappear. It is up to you to treasure them. As Mozart put it, his new ideas came to him in "a pleasing, lively dream." Neil Young's are like wild animals trapped in cages. How and when will yours come to you? And what will you do with them? How do you take full advantage? Two steps.

First, let the whole idea in. Be receptive to its subtleties and nuances, its differences from other ideas you have had. Be welcoming. Don't judge it, just give it some refuge.

Second, capture it entirely. However you can, just do it. Sketch, outline, draft, dictate into a phone, tell somebody, sing it in the shower over and over, film yourself, basically do whatever you have to do, even if it's somewhat embarrassing. It's okay; it's the golden hour and your first responsibility is to grab hold and preserve the *entirety* of the creative burst that just happened.

Television writer and producer Ken Levine tells the story of legend Larry Gelbart, who really knew how to take care of his brand-new ideas. Gelbart started out writing jokes for Sid Caesar and Bob Hope, then developed *M*A*S*H* for television, and won a Tony for the book of *A Funny Thing Happened on the Way to the Forum*. Once, in the middle of the night, Gelbart had an idea exploding in his head and called his secretary, waking her up at her home. He told her to grab a pen, that he had to get the idea out. As he was racing through it, she was falling further and further behind. Finally she said, "You're going too fast, I can't get it all down." He replied, "That's okay, just get half."

Take Full Advantage of the Golden Hour

When the big bang explodes in your head, drop everything. Give over all of yourself to what just happened and embrace the new idea that just appeared. It will be difficult if not impossible to go back in time and try to re-create the inspiration, so get what you can get in that moment.

But suppose you are busy doing something else when your big idea hits. Then what? You can't just leave work, telling your boss, "I'm having an idea. I'll be back in an hour or so." In these cases, you have to condense your golden hour into a golden minute. Even a jerk of a boss would give someone a minute, right? And in that minute, record yourself on your phone, call your voice mail, write a short note with all the key points. Do this as soon as you can, before the idea flies away.

Procrastination is one of the great enemies of creativity, and urgency is one of its great allies. Take full advantage of the first moments in the life of a new idea. Let the urgency inspire you to capture the complete essence of it, and take full advantage of the golden hour.

If you wonder if this guidance contradicts the Babyface Rule (that is, if you can't remember an idea in the morning, then no one else will), it does not. The two actually work together. The golden hour is a tool to use at the very beginning of an idea's life to ensure that you get the most out of each creative burst. Trying to remember that same idea in the morning is a simple test that reveals whether it was memorable or not to begin with.

GIVE EMOTIONAL DIRECTION WITH COLOR

I had graduated from UC Davis with a degree in music, and was attending UCLA to pursue a master's degree in composition and conducting. I was sitting in a graduate music composition class, and another student did something I had never seen before and have never been able to forget. It was remarkably creative and unique, but it was also so simple. She used colors to find the path of emotion she hoped her music would take. She literally colored on the pages before she wrote any music down on them.

Her assignment was to write a movement for a symphony orchestra, to last approximately seven minutes with a full orchestral score. But she did not just present her symphony to the class—she unfurled it, literally. It was twenty-four pages long, all the pages attached side by side, rolled into a banner of her symphonic composition. It stretched all the way across the room, like a carpet runner in a hallway. Of course it was filled with notes and clefs and instructions for all of the players, but it was also covered with colors!

It was blue and orange and purple and all sorts of other hues that swept across the pages. A thin blue line started on page 3 and exploded into a deep-purple ball several sheets later. A series of bright-red circles soon took over, and then these gave way to waves of orange and red. She had let the colors help her guide her creativity by indicating what "feel" or emotion she would want to happen in that section of the piece. She explained that she put the color down first and then created the music to match the color. She started her symphony by imagining the emotional impact she hoped it would have on her audience, and then she created the music that would accompany the colors and accomplish this task.

She picked seven principal emotions, assigned each a color, and gave each color a set of specific musical characteristics. Here is a rough idea of her color guide.

COLOR	EMOTION	LOOK/FEEL
Red	Anger	Conflict, Crashing, Percussive
Pink	Love	Romantic, Lush, Beautiful

Blue	Sadness	Regret, Poignant, Sinuous
Yellow	Happiness	Uplifting, Joyous, Melodic
Green	Hope	Inspirational, Reaching, Triumphant
Purple	Sorrow	Despair, Piercing, Dissonant
Orange	Triumph	Crescendos; Horns; Long, Held Notes

I found it to be such an interesting trick she was playing on herself. She was outlining the emotional journey first and inspiring herself to then create the same feeling in the music. So impressive and memorable was it, I am recommending it here.

One way to inspire your creativity is to assign it an emotional target and then do everything you can to hit that target. Let your creative intellect focus on matching its output to the emotion. Use color to inspire, then let the colors lead the way. Whatever it is that you are working on—inventing a dress for a client to wear at the Academy Awards, designing the atrium of a building, writing a campaign speech, or creating the closing argument of a big trial—let colors guide your intellectual effort. The colors become a mechanism that spring free emotions. The emotions become a mechanism that spring free your creativity.

For example, suppose you wanted a ten-minute speech to start with a few lighthearted anecdotes, followed by a few moments of melancholy, ending with a moment of triumph. Illustrate this first with colors. Take six pages. Across the top of the first two, draw a thick yellow line. Across the top of the next two pages, draw a blue line. On the final two pages, draw an orange line. As you write the speech, follow the colors and, in so doing, keep your intellect focused and targeted, and pointed exactly in the direction that you originally intended to go with the speech.

Though I am not an architect or a poet or many other things I wish I was, this concept of using colors to inspire emotion in order to inspire creativity should apply in those disciplines, just as easily as it did for my fellow student that day at UCLA.

If you are trying to create something impactful and powerful and beautiful and wonderful (and who isn't, frankly), begin with its emotional basis and work up from there. Put the colors in place that match the emotions you want to achieve in the hearts and minds of your audience, then let your creativity design itself around those colors.

HOW A BOLT OF LIGHTNING CAN DEFEAT WRITER'S BLOCK

Many forest fires are started by lightning, more so than all of the other causes combined. There are thousands every year that begin this way, all over the planet. A small bolt of lightning can start one tree smoldering, and the next thing you know, a forest fire is burning.

The creative process is not unlike this. Just as the forest has trees, you have a forest of neurons and synapses. When you have writer's block, your neurons and synapses are just standing around, doing nothing for you. They're not spraying each other, they're not making any connections with one another, they're doing nothing at all! In order to get them back in action, smoking and burning, all you need is a bolt of lightning.

The lightning is someone else's already existing idea! And you can overcome your own creative inertia easily by using a thought that has already worked for someone else, *just to get you started, just to be the bolt of lightning*.

As an example, guitarist Jeff "Skunk" Baxter tells how he gets himself and his cohorts warmed up and ready to record a song. If you do not know him, he was one of the earliest members of two iconic bands, Steely Dan and the Doobie Brothers, playing rhythm guitar for both. He is also on the short list of session guitarists who routinely earn triple scale (three times the union minimum) for their contributions to film scores or artist recordings. To him, a great recording always starts as a great groove. If it does not possess a great beat, or a great "feel," it can't be a great record. So when he needs to get a session started with the right groove, his little bit of lightning is an old Motown Records recording. He asks an engineer to have it play nice and loud, and then he plays along with it on his guitar, and asks his fellow musicians to join him. Maybe it would be a song by Martha and the Vandellas or Smokey Robinson and the Miracles, or the Supremes. He would get his groove started with the existing beat of their hit record, simply by playing along with the track for a few minutes, fitting his guitar sound into their sound, as though he were there in the room where the original recording took place.

When the time was right, and the groove established, he shut off the Motown record and started his own groove, created his own beat, or wrote his own songs. There was a mist of Motown in the air, but he soon made the room and the session his own. It became one of many techniques he used to get the day started, musically speaking. The analogy he used to describe it was like someone in a glider being pulled up into the sky by another plane, though musically speaking it was a song being pulled up into the sky by another song.

Motown music was his bit of lightning. You will have to discover yours. Painters may need to sketch their own version of the hands of the *Mona Lisa* to get things started. Architects may want to draft the rough plans for a Frank Lloyd Wright house. Chefs may challenge themselves to cook up their mom's favorite pasta sauce just to get the pots and pans warmed up.

If you are a lyricist or poet or playwright, or anyone who uses words as part of your creative process, here is some lightning to use as a way to jump-start your creativity. All you really need is a good starting point, and it can be found in the works of someone else, someone very smart and very creative, someone who inspires you. Both *Seven Plays* by Sam Shepard or the *Complete Collected Poems of Maya Angelou* are ideal books for this purpose. Take either book (or any book by an author you love and respect) and randomly open to any page. Without looking too closely, run your finger along that page and stop on *any* line, any line at all.

Wherever you stopped, *that line* becomes the opening line of whatever it is you are creating, whether a short story, a haiku, a screenplay, a memoir—anything with words. The lightning strikes and the creativity will spark to life as you force your intellect to use the borrowed line as if it were your own. All by itself, the line is only the lightning. You have to turn it into a forest fire. And while that one particular line may not survive until the final draft or final edit, its purpose is just to get things started, just enough to help you find your footing again, to help you overcome a momentary intellectual inertia. Yes, it's a trick you are playing on yourself, but not a mean one.

In truth, there is no such thing as writer's block. There is no physical condition (other than trauma or disease) that prevents the hundred billion neurons and hundred trillion synapses from doing what they do most naturally, namely, firing off electrical impulses, spraying excitatory substances, making millions or billions of connections, and accommodating you in your creative process. The brain is simply too enormous for something like writer's block to ever really take control of it.

REGAIN FOCUS WITH DISTRACTION

Shaquille O'Neal is a very creative individual who is always coming up with new ideas, inventions, improvements, product placements, songs ideas, lyrics, samples to interpolate, and video games to play. Several years ago, Shaquille O'Neal and I were on a trip together to the Pacific Rim, promoting music and shoes, stopping in Hong Kong, Taiwan, Singapore, the Philippines, and Australia, among a few other exotic places.

We were promoting his latest album as well as his various brands and artists in a mélange of hype and marketing called Shaq's Rap and Jam Tour, an idea I had come up with. We happened to be in Manila as part of our marketing efforts on this one particular day, and I had arranged for him to visit several of the top radio stations in the city. It turns out there were many "top" radio stations, so by the time we got to the third of the seven planned for that day, he had had enough.

Shaquille has a very interesting personality trait. If you tell him he cannot do something, he will insist upon doing it. And if you tell him he has to do something, he will steadfastly refuse. While Shaquille is great at many things, telling the same stories about himself and what he thinks of Manila over and over was not one of them. And when I told him it was too late in the day to cancel any of the remaining appointments, he was ready to walk out and never walk back in.

For the Manila disc jockeys, meeting an NBA champion and one of the most famous people in the world was a high point of their year. For Shaq, he had almost completely checked out, both intellectually and emotionally, and you could tell by the way he was answering the questions. What should have been amusing anecdotes were quickly becoming monotonic one- or two-word sentences. Good conversation is an exercise in creativity, and the sparring of two intellects is a joy to watch. But this was not that. Right before my eyes he was reverting into an adolescent. To avert disaster, I had to find a way to get him engaged again and enjoying himself.

So we started to play a game, right there in the middle of all the unending interviews—not a basketball-related game, but a word game. It was a way to keep him focused and on track, and on his toes—intellectually speaking. I brought a couple of magazines into the booth and began randomly pointing at words printed inside them. The game was this: I point to a word and he has to use it naturally in the next couple of sentences. If he used that word naturally, correctly, and surreptitiously, he got some points. If he could not use it, he lost some points. However he used it, the word had to sound as if he had just thought of it.

The first few words I chose were easy and fit right into the conversation. But the game grew far more interesting when I pointed to words like "sensational," "instantaneous," "leotard," and "perforated." In the end, he scored a lot of word points and we got through all the interviews. I kept him from losing his mind, we had a few laughs, and I was not locked in a closet somewhere in the outskirts of Manila. Later that night, he played in a basketball game and performed a rap concert at the sold-out Smart Araneta Coliseum, the same place where Muhammad Ali and Joe Frazier fought their way into history with the "Thrilla in Manila."

Keeping Shaquille engaged and interested that day was possible only because his creativity was challenged by the word game. Shaquille is brilliant and his intellect is as agile as a cat, but only by distracting it was I able to keep him interested and engaged in the many conversations we had scheduled for that day. It was a lesson in lion taming, really, but just as much, a lesson in managing creativity.

If you are losing patience or focus or will during the course of your various intellectual efforts, come up with an engaging distraction. Keep your mind both alert and working. It might be as simple as the little word game described above. It might be one of the creative exercises that appear in this book. We learned from Marilyn Bergman and Alan Greenspan that the intellect can operate very well on its own, on several different levels at the same time, without anything but a little guidance and direction. They ask their minds for lyrics or financial solutions while they go for a swim or ride a bike. And you will shortly meet television producer and writer Ken Levine, whose favorite distraction is a long shower.

Anything that distracts works. So it might be the case for you that you need a car ride, a movie, a walk around the block, or anything else that takes your mind completely out of one mode and into another. Possibly, like Shaquille, you will need a good "trick" to play on your intellect to help it keep its attention on the job at hand. Distract it and keep it focused.

LET X MARK THE SPOT AND FIND THE PERFECT DETAIL LATER

Often in the course of creating, the exact right word or phrase or term or analogy, or whatever detail it is that you are looking for, is just not there when you need it. You obviously have not thought of it yet or, for whatever reason, it is otherwise just out of reach. You know roughly what detail you hope to say or write or draw or otherwise include, but you just do not know what it is yet.

Mark that spot with a big X and move on; just keep creating. Do not interrupt the flow of your ideas, the pace of your thinking, the tempo of your thoughts. Do not waste a second waiting for the perfect detail to appear. Trust your mind to find the right word or phrase—*later*—when you are not under pressure and in the middle of transcribing a new idea from your mind to paper or computer. When the bloom or burst of an idea is completed, and the golden hour is over, then you can go back and find the missing word, fix an awkward rhyme, or nuance an analogy until it is sheer perfection.

Possibly an idea has simply disappeared, momentarily, or it is lost in a column of thoughts piled high in your brain somewhere, or it is simply hiding behind another word, somewhere in your mind's millions of unlit streets. It happens.

But this is not just about words; it is about any detail that hides itself in the course of creating: the cornice of a building or the pleat in a suit, a graphic design of a new logo or the look of some advertising copy. Never stop your stream of consciousness simply because a detail has disappeared from sight for a moment. This concept was discussed earlier in relation to Paul McCartney's placeholder for the lyrics of his classic "Yesterday." Instead of an X, he used the words "scrambled eggs." This is the same concept but on a much smaller and more instant basis.

One of creativity's friends is momentum, particularly the momentum of ideas as they tumble out. Do nothing to stop this glorious parade. Let nothing interrupt it. When the burst has subsided, then take a few moments to go back, look for all the X's, and then decide upon the perfect details that eluded you in the heat of the creative moment.

A PEN WITH NO INK IS A THUG

A writing instrument is often asked to play the part of a lifesaver—an idea's lifesaver. You reach out for it, filled with hope and possibility, trying to rescue a thought before it drowns or otherwise slips away forever. You pick it up and that writing instrument sits coolly in your hand, whispering its inviting promise: "I can help you, buddy. . . ." And is there anything worse, frankly, than finding out, too late, that it has no ink? Or that the pencil you grabbed ran out of lead a year ago? Or that you forgot to sharpen it, and who can remember where the sharpener is when you really need it? Or that you forgot to charge your phone and it will not let you dictate your latest perfect idea? Is there anything more frustrating and distracting to the creative process than these distractions? Instead of the satisfaction of performing a rescue on it, you sit there gritting your teeth while some wonderful idea saunters off, possibly never to be seen again.

A pen with no ink is a thug in a dark alley. A computer that will not boot up instantly is an assassin. An unsharpened pencil is like a shoe bomb. Whatever it is that you use to help you capture your creativity, you have to be sure it is ready when you are.

Have you got a minute? Check that cup full of pens and throw out the bad ones. All those stubby pencils? Get rid of them, too. If your iPad or tablet needs a couple of minutes to get ready, those couple of minutes could cost you dearly. Figure out how to keep it at the ready.

If your creative workspace is cluttered and crowded by little sticky notes and filled-up yellow pads, clean up a little. Buy some manila folders and organize the place. Clutter is a slippery stepping-stone right in the middle of your creative path. It could easily distract you, just as a beautiful idea is coming into focus. Get rid of it and anything else that might get in your way.

Every pen should be full of ink and available, your pencils sharpened and at attention. Empty note pads and reams of paper should be in plain sight, ready to be filled with new ideas. Computers should be frequently serviced and backed up regularly—the very last thing you want is a file to go missing or be compromised by poor maintenance.

Whatever it is that you are creating, ensure that your writing instruments and the environment in which you dream this stuff up do not have the chance to prevent you from capturing the best of your ideas. Ensure that the tools of your creativity are as prepared as you are.

You never know just when or how an idea will come to you. Be ready for anything.

THE LONG AND GRINDING ROAD

Songwriters will often talk about working all afternoon on a song and getting absolutely nowhere with it, but at the end of the session, when they switch to something else, a great idea emerges and in twenty minutes a brand-new song is finished. It is probably *not* the song they set out to write but possibly something more beautiful and more successful.

The creative mind can be elusive. It cannot be coerced. It cannot be forced to act. You can feed it with inspirations and obligations and fill every cup in the room with freshly sharpened pencils and you still might get absolutely nothing in return.

This is the intellect acting as a natural filter. This is your mind guarding against creations that might not deserve to be created—inventions that do not deserve patents, Broadway musicals that should stay in the trunk, buildings that should never get built. Yes, do treat every idea like a good idea, with respect for its possibilities and promise. But not every idea is a great idea.

Just because you came up with the seed of something does not require that you give it years of your time, and six drafts, and the right to be a completed work. While Mark Zuckerberg was creating Facebook, my friend Lou and I created the Executive Door Closer, a device that closes office doors by remote control. We probably spent as much time and money as Mr. Zuckerberg did, at least at the beginning. Mr. Zuckerberg's idea is connecting the world and is now worth hundreds of billions of dollars. The Executive Door Closer Company went out of business and Lou recently took the few remaining units to a scrap yard. I should have listened to my intellect when it was shouting out, over and over, "Hey, stupid, this is *not* a winner." But I thought the long and grinding road was a sign that we just needed to keep persevering. Wrong. We were smarter about some of our other ideas, however, and wisely let them disappear, and this is why you will never ride a RollerBoggan (a toboggan on wheels) or hang your raincoat on a Portable Hat Rack (it has only two feet and leans against walls). You will never read "Hip-Hop Chronicles" (graphic novels based on old rap songs), and you will never watch a TV show called "I Write the Songs" (an *American Idol*–for-songwriters idea I had). I spent countless hours walking the long and grinding road for all of these unsatisfying projects, using millions of precious synaptic connections in the process—all for nothing.

So does this guideline contradict my earlier recommendations? Does it conflict with Diane Warren's showing up every day at 8:30 a.m. no matter what happened the night before, for instance? Hardly. Being tenacious and unrelenting with your creative spirit, as Diane is, is different from trying to force your creativity to deliver a result that it simply cannot deliver. She does not demo, pitch, pray, and grind for every song she starts, and she knows when it's time to turn to something else. Even she cannot find gold where there is only granite.

Sometimes your intellect will not cooperate with you for a good reason, namely because it might not be such a great project to begin with. You will know you are in the middle of one of these conundrums when your teeth grit and you emit a heavy sigh just at the thought of getting back to work on it. So why burn all that time and effort? Why fry all those synapses and waste all that excitatory brain fluid? The lack of response on the part of your intellect may simply be your creative instinct advising you that no more is available for this particular project at this particular time.

Forcing creativity is not a great use of your intellect and will eliminate much of the joy that creativity should bring. When you find yourself going back and back again to the same problem, and always coming out with the same frustration, let it go. The definition of insanity is to do the same thing over and over while hoping for a different outcome. So if you find yourself forcing the same creative issue again and again, and teetering on the edge of your sanity, leave that mess behind you and find another more satisfying project to devote yourself to.

Do not delete or erase or throw away these unfinished treasures. Just let them go, for now, and hope you get a chance to be inspired by them again another day.

A TABLE OF CONTENTS AS A CREATIVE TOOL

Often in creating, you can get lost in a thicket of your ideas. You can forget exactly what you were hoping to achieve in a particular section of a speech, or misremember why you used a particularly oblique analogy, or lose the train of thought that put the stairs in the kitchen of the house you were designing, for instance.

For whatever creative project you might be working on, particularly if it is something big and long and complicated, a table of contents will be a blueprint from which you can more easily and readily assess and evaluate the quality of your efforts.

A table of contents will allow you an overview that is both flexible and easy to understand. It is also a nudging reminder that you may have veered off track in a particular section of your efforts. And a table of contents is very easy to change if you want to give your project a different look or send it off in a different direction.

By way of example, if you write out a draft of the

table of contents at the same time that you begin to write the first few pages of your book, they will grow together and you can maintain the direction that inspired you in the first place. If you draft a list of all the songs in your musical theater piece and let it serve as your table of contents, this list will keep you on track while you finish the script. The table of contents, like a thesis does for a term paper, keeps the focus of the piece in view.

A table of contents functions on your behalf as a creative tool in these five ways:

1. It reminds you what work still needs to be done on your project
2. It allows you to look at your project from a sobering and healthy distance in order to make the changes necessary to keep on the right track
3. It encourages you to recognize the superfluous and delete an idea or section of your project if it no longer has the same value it did when you originally created it. There is always settling that occurs after a project starts to take on some heft, and ideas that you could not imagine living without may be trumped by better ideas that came along subsequently. The table of contents allows you to see this more easily.

4. It serves as a finish line and points you to the conclusion of a draft

5. It constantly reminds you of the original intent and purpose of your creative project

CREATIVITY'S FRIENDS AND ENEMIES

If creativity finds a place in your life, it will only be so because you are certain and willing and welcoming of its right to be there. You show this in simple ways, like when the urge to create hits you and you stop everything and respond to it. Or when a new idea appears and you give it life and refuge within its first hour, before your synapses rearrange themselves and think of something else. Or if a collaborator comes up with something brilliant and you are able to recognize that brilliance and respond to it as though it were your own.

There are things that bolster your creativity, and support it, and encourage it to return again and again for more good times. And on the other hand, there are things that diminish it and your ability to use it whenever you need it. For the sake of simplicity, I have called these the "friends and enemies of creativity." I ask you to note which are in your world already that you are using to maximize your creative power,

and which are in your life still that should be elimi-
nated at the first opportunity.

Friends of Creativity

Confidence

A long walk

Momentum

A quiet place to think

Inspiration

A meaningful deadline

Patience

If you doubt its purpose and place, creativity will
race right out of your life. Failure to show complete
confidence in your creativity will minimize any
chance you have of engaging it on a regular basis.
Here are several things that can prevent your successful creating.

Enemies of Creativity

Doubt

Fear

Self-consciousness

Needless distractions and clutter

Pens with no ink

Negative collaborators

Judgmental friends (who always mean well)

Distractions

As you are thinking about ways to gain greater satisfaction and results from your creative efforts, consider the lasting value of this guideline. When you surround your creativity with its friends, you treat it like it belongs with you and is a part of your life. When you show your creativity your complete respect, you will get that much more from it.

As soon as you can, dismiss the enemies—before they get comfortable in your life.

CREATIVE EXERCISE #5

A Caption Contest

❖❖❖

This is a creative exercise that can take many unexpected turns and many creative twists. There is an element of collaboration as well as competition, but more than anything else this is an opportunity for creativity to strut and flourish. You can play with a partner against others, or by yourself against some other equally reckless individual. Or, if no one is around, you can play against yourself.

Start with any photo or drawing that shows a circumstance that needs either a lot of explaining or very little explaining: two nuns walking out of a bar, a car parked half off a pier dangling over the water, an eagle and a cat eyeing each other through a small opening, etc. Or simply draw two heads, one smiling and the other miserable. Then create the caption that would appear underneath. It can be a description or dialogue, whichever you like. As long as it's funny, or tries to be.

This exercise is actually taken from the *New Yorker* magazine cartoon caption contest. The magazine does it every week as a way of engaging its readers and turning the magazine experience into something more interactive than scratching and sniffing the perfume samples. (Visit newyorker.com/caption contest for some examples.)

The exercise here is obviously to come up with the best caption or to improve on the one that just came before, until the funniest or most poignant or most meaningful one is found. When the photo or drawing is all used up, move on and let the next contest begin.

COLLABORATIVE GROUP
CREATIVITY

THE FIRST FIVE CHAPTERS OF THIS BOOK
discuss several aspects of creativity that
focus primarily on one's individual relationship with the creative process.

But creativity is not always practiced in the splendor of solitude, and it is not always an individual
sport. Creative projects often require teamwork: collaborations among songwriters, screenwriters, architects, advertising agency execs, party planners, or
trial lawyers. The ability to collaborate with other
people will often mean the difference between the

success or failure of any given project. Teams can also be husband and wife, teacher and students, or two strangers caught in an elevator trying to get to safety.

Collaborative creativity is a very different process from the kind we practice by ourselves. Learning to respect the ideas of others demands great compassion. Learning to watch others succeed and fail requires great patience. Learning to exchange ideas freely with others in a collaborative or group context demands great confidence in your own ability and a trust that your compatriots will not shower you with ridicule.

The guidelines that follow provide a basic framework for creativity in a collaboration. They are meant to give you an understanding of working more successfully and effectively as a teammate in a partnership, or as one of a group of creators, all pushing toward a common creative solution.

These ideas are intended to provide you stepping-stones and building blocks. You will walk into collaborations better prepared. You will have more certainty as to what is expected of you and what role you might be asked to play in a particular circumstance. You will know that you and everyone else have the right to "expect to be respected."

Collaborative creativity is all about the whole of

you being greater than the sum of your individual parts, giving everyone involved the right to expect great things of themselves and all the other members of the group.

MAKE A RIDICULE-LESS PROMISE

Before anyone begins creating anything in a collaborative situation, everyone in the group must be on the same page with regard to what rules will guide the collaborative experience. The most important of all of these is for all participants to make a promise to everyone else in the group that no one will be ridiculed, made fun of, diminished, damned with faint praise, or in any other way reduced by the experience of working together.

The promise should be made out loud, by the whole room, to the whole room, in front of everyone, with lots of witnesses to attest that it was said, so that there is no going back and so that it is that much easier to remind someone who has broken the promise to get back in line. This promise will ensure that every voice in the room is heard, not just those of the brazen, fearless, type A alpha males and females. The promise will encourage a vitally important "no-fear" zone within the group and should last for however long the project lasts, whether it is a few hours, a few days, a few weeks, or however long. This does not mean that everyone participating has to like every idea he or she hears, it simply means ideas will not be ridiculed on their way out into the world.

As discussed a little earlier, I have had the great privilege of teaching creativity as a skill to more than a thousand public school students in the LAUSD (Los Angeles Unified School District) and the MBUSD (Manhattan Beach Unified School District). The key to making the process work for children of all ages is to give the students the right to be fearless in the face of the creativity that is unleashed all around them. One of the best moments happens at the beginning of each class, when I ask every student to look into the eyes of another student across the room and repeat after me the following: "I will not laugh at your ideas . . . unless they are funny!" This somehow gives everyone the freedom to be themselves and to laugh when something strikes them as hilarious, which somehow always happens, by the way.

One television producer who you will meet shortly solved the problem by insisting that a sign be placed on the wall of any room in which he was working with a group of writers. It read: NO LIFE-SHORTENING EVENTS WILL TAKE PLACE HERE. This is a great guideline to follow in any room where creativity and collaboration are expected to mix.

Another way to ensure that the environment stays healthy and "ridicule-less" is to have everyone who is participating write down on a piece of paper the promise of no ridicule, sign it, and then put all the pieces of paper in a pile in the middle of the table. If someone's tone or manner begins to cross the line, everyone else can point to the promises in the paper pile.

The freedom to create without ridicule is the basis and foundation of any successful collaborative group activity. It allows for courage to bloom, and without courage and fearlessness there can be no real successful creativity. Participants, whether two or twenty, will give more of their best if they are certain that there will be no snickering or levity accompanying the presentation of their ideas, unless they're funny!

The purpose of the group working together is to have the creativity in the room build on itself and on the creativity of others in the room. Creativity creates its own momentum, and given the freedom to be creative without any friction or diminishment, the chances are stronger that the room will deliver bigger and better ideas, more unusual possibilities, more visualization of things that have never been seen before, and ultimately more solutions to the group's creative mission, whatever it happens to be.

CHOOSE A LEADER

There needs to be a leader who everyone accepts as the leader. If there is no leader, there will be chaos. The leader will make or guide the final decisions about where the project is headed, discover and maintain the pace and purpose of the room, and keep everyone adhering to the various creativity-inducing promises that will be required for the room to enjoy any success. In a TV writers' room, the leader is called the show runner, and this person is ultimately responsible to the production company that is paying the bills. He or she is expected to maintain the pace and deliver on the output. In a few pages, you will meet four successful show runners and learn how each ran the room.

The leader must have great people skills and great instincts in understanding the project he or she is being asked to lead. A humorless person would fail as the leader of a sitcom writers' room; someone with a limited imagination would fail at trying to guide a team of architects to come up with a bridge or a building. At the same time, if the person is very nice but intends to serve as the grammar police or a clock watcher, the session will likely fail as well.

The leader has many responsibilities, including having the final word on which ideas are preserved and which are cast to the side. He or she must compliment the ideas that appear, and guide the room's reaction to them and inspiration from them, but not be afraid to reject or otherwise table them. The individual must always be focused, concentrating on the task at hand. Most important, this person has to be able to ask great questions, lead the discussion that answers the questions, and pick the answers that solve the problems under discussion.

Unfortunately in business, the role of leader usually belongs to, or is rewarded to, the most senior executive, and this is often the last person who should have such responsibility. I had one boss who led a biweekly creative meeting by plodding through an agenda and shushing people who went off topic or out of order. To any idea that did not suit his very conservative style, he would wave it away and say, "That's just wacky! Next . . ." Needless to say, those creative meetings were anything but.

So how does a creative group pick a leader? Find someone suited for the task, a team builder who can pick the route and set the pace. Analogous to a jury picking the foreman, the team should elect its leader and follow his or her direction. Leadership is expected, and his or her decisions, at least for that day or that session, will be considered the final decisions. The person will be living between two extremes: idea cheerleader and idea executioner. If you know you're not right for the position, don't volunteer.

WARM UP

It is naive and foolish and too much to hope that a group of people can suddenly begin to create. The mind just does not work that way. The muse does not make or take any appointments. He or she appears, at his or her leisure, and disappears just as quickly. Almost like at a séance, creativity must be inspired to appear. It will begin only when it is ready to begin.

Throughout this book, I have laid out five creative exercises. These are ideal to begin any group creativity session. I have had the opportunity to test each of them on numerous occasions, whether while teaching a class in creativity or discussing the subject during a lecture. If you want to get a room full of people to pay attention to you, and to start thinking quicker and smarter, start playing the Excellent Question Game. If you want to get your team focused on a complex problem that needs understanding and then fixing, come to understand it better by warming up with Reductions and More Reductions. A Caption Contest will lighten the mood of any group, as will If You Were Someone Else, How Would You Think?

You would not step onto a tennis court for a big match, or play a round of golf, or go for a long run without stretching your legs and back thoroughly. You risk injuring muscles that have not been prepared to conquer the task at hand. Creativity deserves the same preparation. Warm up your intellect before you ask it to work for you.

Many of these warm-up exercises are also effective in the middle of a session when you need to reboot or refocus your group's attention.

ONCE AROUND THE TABLE

One of the best opening moves in a group creativity situation, especially if it's conceptual and in the early stages, is to go once around the table with no interruptions. Everyone participating has a chance to state their opening ideas—with the full attention of all the other participants at the table, waiting their turn to speak. You will learn much about your teammates, how they think and how they speak, and how well they are prepared to accomplish the task at hand.

Much will be revealed. Those who are shy will be quieter. Those who are arrogant will be more so as well. Once around the table is like a crucible that exaggerates the best and worst of those sitting in it.

SILENCE INSTEAD OF "NO"

Is there a stronger word than the word *no* in a creative situation? No, there is not. Nothing stops an idea in its tracks like that word. A loud "Noooo" is a rain cloud in the middle of a beautiful family picnic. If you want to watch an idea shriek and run away, just yell "No!" at its creator. That idea will likely disappear forever, as will several measures of lingering hope in the person who thought enough of their idea to bring it up to the group.

"No" is unfairly judgmental in group creativity. An idea is tainted by it. "No" builds nothing. It does not inspire any other ideas in anyone else's head, so why use it?

Songwriters who sit back and say no to their collaborators' ideas are rarely invited back for another session, and for this reason alone they rarely have any hits in their catalogs, if they have any catalogs at all. In office settings, you will often hear the word "no." "No" people are the ones who will explain, often in rich detail, precisely why an idea or plan or suggestion will never work, even before the whole idea is presented. They are usually shaking their heads from side to side as they pretend to listen, proving that they played judge, jury, and executioner of the idea before it even came out into the world. Meetings with "no" people frequently come to a dead stop right after the "no" person speaks, until someone finally says, "Anyway . . ." These individuals rarely realize that their habit is their weakness, and their inability to let a new idea live, even for a few moments, is why they are invited to fewer and fewer meetings.

To get the best out of a collaboration, everyone participating must feel that they can bring up any idea without judgments getting in the way. Nothing says judgment louder or more clearly than "no."

Instead of saying no to an idea, try silence. Silence is such a good option. Remind and re-remind and then encourage your group to say absolutely nothing if there is nothing good to say. It was Thumper's mother in *Bambi* who taught him, "If you can't say somethin' nice, don't say nothin' at all." If you cannot think of a response that would qualify as either a compliment or an improvement, then just keep your thoughts to yourself. If silence was ever really golden, it would be at a creative moment like this. Possibly the person speaking has a great and wonderful idea just a little farther down the idea column, and it's right there underneath the not-so-great ones. And if no one interrupts with a "no" or a long sigh, possibly that idea will have time to emerge.

There is a Sicilian aphorism on this very topic that my Sicilian father-in-law, Professor Sam Armato, encourages me to live by. In Italian it sounds something like *Un pesce muore con la boca aperta*, which translates very roughly as, "A fish dies with its mouth open." If you can just keep your mouth closed, you do yourself no harm. And nowhere does this wisdom apply with more purchase than in a setting meant to inspire group creativity.

A little silence goes a long way in these situations.

LEAVE EGOS AT THE DOOR

Most people are incredibly sensitive about their creative turf and react poorly to any comment that is not complimentary or phrased just right. In a group creativity situation, there are probably going to be more comments that are uncomplimentary than there will be compliments. In any collaboration, both sides— the presenter and the listener(s)—have to feel free to listen and process and make suggestions and *not* be won over by an idea.

So there must be a predetermined arrangement among all the participants in the group creativity or collaborative situation, whether among a group of marketing executives, a team of architects, teacher and students, creators and mentor, big sisters and little brothers, or conductor and orchestra: everyone has to leave their ego at the door. Repeat: everyone has to leave their ego at the door. As part of the ground rules, the fundamental agreement must be that all opinions are welcome, positive or negative, praising or suggesting, complimentary or rudimentary. All reactions, as long as they are honest, have a right to be aired, as long as they are done with kindness and respect. Sadly, people with easily bruised egos and inflated self-worth have a difficult time in a collaboration or group creativity situation. Unlike Carole King, they are unable or unwilling to ask for and then show proper consideration to the opinions of others.

By participating in the room, or the project,

everyone has to agree on this point. People need to feel that they can contribute without fear of bumping into the next guy's ego. A polite rejection can sometimes advance the cause of the room brilliantly, and everyone has to know that if an idea is rejected, maybe that was its contribution.

In one of the creativity classes I taught at a Los Angeles public school, the assignment I gave to a group of twenty-five students was to write a song collectively, as a group, and then I took them to a recording studio together to record a demo. As things got under way, the song was practically creating itself. This was mainly due to the contributions of one of the girls in the group who was not only full of great ideas but fearless about presenting them. When we needed it most, she consistently came up with a winner of a line, or analogy, or an idea that inspired another idea in someone else. She ended up studying at one of the top universities in the country, and if she does not become a poet or a writer or a novelist at some point, I would be very surprised.

But even despite her prolific creativity there was a problem. As she presented her ideas, it became very clear that she had no singing voice whatsoever. She wrote beautiful lyrics and had inspirational ideas, yes, but her voice was neither beautiful nor inspiring.

Even though many of the lyrics we recorded were hers, we were unable to use her voice as part of the recording. I asked her to join me in the control room and very privately told her why she needed to sing more quietly. I reminded her of her many significant contributions to the song and complimented her for all of them. My strongest memory of the experience is her bravely smiling and wiping a tear from a freckled cheek, saying that it was all fine and that she understood completely. She told me she had always thought hers was not a great voice, and she thanked me for allowing her to contribute in the way that she had, so she could shine and be at her best.

She left her ego at the door. And everyone benefited as a result. The song turned out to be a beautiful little tune called "A Message of Hope for Maria," which was written to encourage a young cancer victim to continue her fight against leukemia.

RESPONDING TO NEW IDEAS

The response to any new idea is very important in enabling creativity in these kind of rooms. In a group creativity situation, there are several workable reactions to hearing a new idea as it is presented. Earlier we discussed the eternal peace brought about by reacting with complete silence, and this is often the best bet, especially if you cannot come up with any of the following.

First, offer a simple compliment. "Good idea." "Nice concept." "Great starting point." An uncontrived compliment recognizes the *fact* of the new idea's arrival without standing in judgment of it. It must be truthful and meaningful but not solicitous.

Second, suggest an improvement that does not require the entire idea be changed top to bottom. For instance, you say, "How about what John just said, but suppose the dogs fly instead of driving race cars?" Or, "Can we do the same basic idea, only make it less dangerous?" Or, "Can we do the same idea, only a lot more dangerous?" In other words, take some of the good from the idea and build on it in the same general direction.

Third, use the idea that was just presented as a jumping-off point and change the course of the discussion somewhat. Veer off the main road but stay within shouting distance. Go wherever you want to go, regardless of where things were before you started. This is a most challenging way to proceed within the confines of group creativity, but it might also be the most interesting. You can save the room a lot of time and energy by sparking new ideas in everyone else's head, but only if the room allows you to make the change.

Fourth, ignore the previous idea completely and offer something that is unexpected and unapologetic, and almost completely random. Push the group in an entirely new direction. At best, it's a complete non sequitur; at worst, it's a complete surprise. It will either anger or inspire the others in the group and this, too, will be good, as another new idea may just burst through.

THE LESS CROSS TALK THE BETTER

Once collaborative group creativity gets under way, sooner or later there will be mayhem. Ideas will fly around the room, insights and epiphanies will overwhelm some participants, and the air will be heavy with fresh thoughts. Distractions will rule the moment as ideas run around the place like cats after mice. People will laugh because they'll hear something funny, or remark to the person sitting next to them that the guy in the white suit looks like Colonel Sanders. A good simile will break into the clearing and possibly inspire ten others. There is no way to stop any of this. It is part of the magic. But without some modicum of order, the functionality of your group will disappear.

One way to establish some semblance of order is to make a general rule that all conversation and exchange of ideas should take place within the group of you sitting there. Ask everyone to try to avoid cross talk, private jokes, testing an idea on the lady next to you to see if it is ready for the whole room to hear, etc. Like a turbo engine that turns its exhaust into more power, you must try to ensure that all of the ideas that the room creates stay in the room, are enjoyed and discussed by the entire group, and gather a creative momentum on behalf of the entire group.

If an idea slips away into a private conversation instead of being part of the group creativity process, its absence diminishes the ultimate outcome the group might have been able to accomplish. Thus, there can be no cross talk. Keep everything in the room and everyone on the same page. Keep all the oars pulling in the same direction, sharing every idea with everyone in the room.

Encourage every question and every idea to be discussed by *everyone*. This can happen only if people are not having private conversations. Share an idea or oblique reference or analogy, or something interesting or something funny—with every other person in the room, not just one or two. The whole point of the group creativity and the adventure everyone is taking together is that it is *together*, that everyone has ideas as a group, as a team of creators.

IF YOU CANNOT LAND A HAYMAKER, BE A COUNTERPUNCHER

In the next chapter you will be introduced to TV writer and producer Allan Burns. He collaborated on the creation of one of the most seminal shows in television, *The Mary Tyler Moore Show*. Burns was a member of the writing team for *Room 222*, when he and another contributor, James L. Brooks, were approached by legendary television producer and executive Grant Tinker. Tinker was looking for a TV vehicle for his wife, who had just completed her star turn in *The Dick Van Dyke Show*.

In the days and weeks that followed, Burns and Brooks met several times, and a pattern of creativity was established between them. Brooks came up with a lot of the big ideas, jumping in the air with enthusiasm and excitement about something he had just thought of, always swinging for the fences, always trying to land his big ideas. Brooks was always throwing "these wild haymakers," as they were described by his collaborator. Burns found himself sitting back and listening, shaping the idea, finding a nuance that worked, staying out of the way while chipping away at some grandiose scheme until it became something they could work with going forward. He described his role in the team as being the "counterpuncher." More thoughtful and more considered, he reacted to the ideas rather than originating them. He would often provide the perfect detail to accompany the broad stroke, the shimmy to Brooks's shake. This balancing act was not a constant in all of their collaborations, but simply a detail Burns recalled about several of their early meetings.

In your own collaborations, find the part you want to play. If you are full of huge ideas, throw them in the middle of the room and see how they fare. If you are better at reacting to ideas than creating them, know that about yourself as well, and contribute the best you can under the circumstances. As long as you are speaking your own truth, whether you land the haymakers or the counterpunches, know that both efforts have great value in the collaboration.

WHO'S THE BOSS—AND WHO CARES?

Getting everyone in the room or in the collaboration on equal footing is not so easy. In business there are hierarchies, in entertainment there is pedigree, in law firms there are partners, and in almost every circumstance there are going to be overly confident alpha types. But if the collaboration or group creativity is to be successful, everyone participating must feel that he or she stands on equal footing with everyone else, that no one has a higher place to rest, that there is no pecking order.

Here's a technique to help illustrate the equality of all the participants. Everyone in the room takes a small piece of paper and writes on it his or her title, or great achievement, or other raison d'être for being there in the first place. All the slips of paper are then gathered in an envelope or small box, or just a pile, and placed in the middle of the table. This action symbolizes that, for these next few moments, at least, there is no rank, there are no bosses, there is no pyramid of power, there is no reason for anyone present to feel diminished by anyone else present. This is an inducement for all to put forward only their very best ideas into the group collaboration.

In group creativity, who really cares who the boss is? In this kind of room, where everyone acts with creative purpose, the boss is the one with the best ideas.

THE SLASH

A simple, easy-to-use transition device in group creativity is the slash. It connects one idea to another, regardless of how far apart the ideas actually are. Think of it as a rickety bridge.

Say that a roomful of advertising executives is trying to sell more beer in China. Ad exec number one starts off and pitches his idea, which is boring and just like every other beer ad. "It's set in a bar near a college and everybody is having a great time drinking big pitchers of our beer." Ad exec number one looks around the room for approbation and sees only blank looks. Ad exec number two sits up and says, "Slash . . . they're dressed like college students, in T-shirts and shorts, except they're all fire-breathing dragons." Ad exec number three practically flies out of his seat and yells, "Fire-*fighting* fire-breathing dragons just having a beer after saving the local forest." Ad exec number four sees an opening, and says, ". . . which was likely set by this one dragon who has allergies. Every time he sneezes he sets something on fire, and he keeps setting things in the bar on fire." Ad exec number two says, "Then one dragon turns to another and says, 'Is it hot in here, or is it me?' Ad exec number five, the youngest of the group, who has been sitting quietly while all this transpires, and who happens to be from St. Louis, finally says, "Slash . . . lights go down, spotlight comes up. And there's the rapper Nelly up on a stage as himself, performing "It's Getting Hot in Here (So Take off All Your Clothes)." Everybody loves this idea, particularly ad exec number one, who is thrilled that his idea started off the whole conflagration.

That's the slash and how you can use it to present any idea, regardless of how random or nonsequential it might sound at first, without diminishing or disrespecting any of the other participants in your group creativity session.

YES, AND . . .

Another transitional device that can be used to walk a non sequitur into the discussion comes from the world of improvisational comedy. When these actors are interacting with one another, the number one rule they must follow is to keep things moving, keep the ideas flowing, keep the ball in the air. The words "Yes, and . . ." provide them with a transition between *any* two ideas.

COLLABORATIVE GROUP
CREATIVITY IN ACTION:
THE TV WRITERS' ROOM

I HAD ALWAYS IMAGINED THAT THE WRITERS' rooms of hit comedy TV shows had to be the most creative and collaborative rooms in the world. I thought that they would have to be the kinds of gatherings where writers would scheme and dream, and try to make sense out of life while trying to make one another laugh. I pictured packs of unique individuals, both very troubled and very funny, sitting together every day to find humor in a world that could hardly find itself. This was all just a beautiful fantasy until I had the opportunity to interview several writers, producers, and show runners who had actually participated in some of the most iconic and longest-running television sitcoms in the history of the medium.

Thanks to television director Jay Sandrich (*Get Smart, The Odd Couple, Soap,* and many others), I was able to meet the creators of *The Mary Tyler Moore Show*; *The Cosby Show*; the head writer of *M*A*S*H*, who also wrote for *Cheers* and *Frasier*; and the creator and show runner for *thirtysomething*. Thanks to Allan Burns, I was introduced to the creator of *Taxi* and *The Simpsons*, who is a three-time Academy Award–winning writer and director. The wisdom shared by these individuals is miles past unforgettable when it comes to managing and understanding group creativity. In many cases, these are people who spent the best years of their lives creating the best that television has ever had to offer.

My fantasy image of the writers' room paled in comparison to the reality of the lives and careers of the individuals who flourished there. What they described were perfect expressions of group creativity and collaboration. Under pressures of time and circumstance, with a large group of unique personalities, the rooms had to create interesting, heartfelt, funny stories, week after week after week—for years.

They were required to engage their creativity on a regular and repeatable basis, just to earn a living. Obviously, they were not ordinary people by any means, and even so, it was not easy to keep a seat in the rooms in which they plied their trade. But somehow they did and in many cases continue to do so. There is no rule book for how to make a television show successful and funny, and keep it successful and funny. That's because it's such an individual approach. There is very little science and a great deal of art involved. There are a few practiced methodologies and a great deal of constantly changing improvisations. Each producer runs his or her room in a unique way, very differently from other producers. Of course there are similar overarching ideals that each of them follow, but the magic is in the details of their various approaches.

What follows are the essential elements of successful collaborative group creativity according to several of the most successful writers and producers in television. This is their understanding of how to build a place where any number of creative people can create, free from the chaos of criticism, unafraid to open their hearts.

No matter how you go about creating, especially in a collaboration or large group-think situation, the rules that run the TV writers' rooms will provide you with several workable guidelines that will enable your group's creativity to come forth in ways that you never thought possible.

JOHN MARKUS

John Markus was the Emmy-winning creator and producer of one of the most successful shows in television, *The Cosby Show*. He wrote more than seventy episodes of the groundbreaking sitcom. He also worked extensively as a writer and producer on *The Larry Sanders Show*. He is a gentle and understanding man who tries to bring out the best in everyone with whom he works and plays. He believes that the tone of the television writers' room is set by the show runner, the person who picks the writers, issues clear parameters for their creative interaction, and guides the process by which new episodes are created. He knows well how ideas are best exchanged among the participants in the room.

Markus believes that the relationship of all the participants in the writers' room is no different from any other human relationship. There has to be a flow and an honest exchange based first and foremost on respect. For his writers' room to climb the mountain week after week, the tone in the room needs to reinforce the respect writers have for one another and their ideas. Writers must be able to completely trust the room, because in it they will open their hearts and say over and over, "What do you think?" A harsh statement or an unkind phrase is a joke killer and the death of passion. So there must not be negative judgments. The purpose of the room is to evolve and improve an idea or group of ideas.

One major influence on Markus's process and management of writers comes from working with Bill Cosby for many years. With Cosby, praise was rare. When *The Cosby Show* won an Emmy for Best Comedy on Television one year, Cosby, in his thank-you speech, never mentioned his writers. When Markus objected to being overlooked, Cosby said, "Next time someone asks me about the writers, I'll say they're just fine."

Apparently working with Jackie Gleason was no picnic, either. Jackie Gleason was as nasty to his writers as any star has ever been. He would rehearse his lines from the front seats of his theater with a martini in one hand and a cigarette in the other. After rehearsal, writers would get a note under their doors telling them to tighten jokes or rewrite scenes.

Writers knew they couldn't get Gleason to buy into an idea unless he was in a good mood. Stationed all around the golf course he owned and played every morning were primitive mobile phones. The writers would wait for the caddy to tell them Gleason got a par or birdie, and then pitch him an idea.

Summarizing what is required to get the room right and still keep the star happy, John Markus said in our interview. "Whoever they are, you've got to keep the jerks out of the room or they will pervade and kill. Defensive people become toxic and change the balance of the room. They are less trusting and more suspicious." He went on, "The writers' room is sometimes like group therapy, and a mob mentality can take place if someone is withholding their truth. When creating a new episode of a successful show, the factor of difficulty is so high. By trying to achieve greatness every moment, you have to have kindness abounding."

To Markus, the room has to be a safe place where people feel free to be vulnerable and trusting. There can be no snickering, no humiliation or embarrassment. The writers in the writers' room practice the craft of making something as good as it can possibly be. Humor is 95 percent surprise and, in the words of

Bill Cosby, sometimes you need to surprise people with the obvious. Creativity, to John Markus, is a fragile thing. Like psychiatry, it's also an archaeological dig. He says, "You have to get people to take out all the broken vases and see where they fit on the shelf of life."

John Markus's Rules of the Writers' Room

- There are no junior people, no lesser people
- The idea has the weight, not the person. The room must see past rank.
- No prejudice or bias against whoever had the idea
- What is exchanged in the writers' room is the riches of that room
- Kindness, to yourself and others, is the key to the room's success
- The two most important words spoken in the writers' room are "Yes, and . . ."

John Markus's Tools of the Writers' Room

- Kindness
- Respect
- Patience
- Listening

JAMES L. BROOKS

If anyone knows the TV writers' room, how to run one and how to keep it from running itself into the ground, it would be James L. Brooks. He has been a mainstay of comedic television for the last forty years, almost without cessation. He began as a writer in the 1960s on shows like *That Girl*, *My Mother the Car*, and *The Andy Griffith Show*. He teamed up with Allan Burns and they created and wrote *Room 222*, *The Mary Tyler Moore Show*, *Rhoda*, and *Lou Grant*. On his own, Brooks then created and executive produced *Taxi*.

He made the almost impossible transition to motion pictures, producing, writing, and directing *Terms of Endearment*, *Broadcast News*, and *As Good As It Gets*. He also served as producer of *War of the Roses*, *Jerry Maguire*, and *Big*.

But he also stayed in television, and in 1987 helped create *The Tracy Ullman Show*. He executive produced eighty episodes, during which time he encouraged Matt Groening to develop some animated sketches to play into commercials. These sketches, based loosely on Groening's dysfunctional family, soon became the longest-running animated show in TV history, *The Simpsons*. Brooks has been executive producer of every episode, in addition to co-writing and producing the *Simpsons Movie*. According to IMDB, he has been nominated for fifty-seven different awards and won forty-four times, including three Oscars and nineteen Emmys.

We met years ago when he helped fund the Preston Sturges Reading Room at the Writers Guild of America headquarters, and thanks to Allan Burns, we spoke recently about Mr. Brooks's own creative efforts, and the TV writers' room as a template for collaborative group creativity.

He described his own creative process, after a long pause to consider the answer, as "The spending of self, to end with something you end up serving to others." He uses two distinctly different types of creativity: individual writing, as for his motion picture screenplays, and Group Think writing, which he uses in writers' rooms. He says that different muscles get involved. "Different everything when it's a group effort. You can afford to be patient when you're by yourself. Television is deadlines . . ."

One way *The Simpsons* meets its many deadlines is by having two writers' rooms—a smaller one and a larger one. The smaller room, with typically just three participants, is the high level. They discuss the direction of the episode, the "ambition" of the show to be delivered that week. The larger room, with many funny writers in it, then jumps down into the weeds and comes up with the specific dialogue lines, jokes, and stumbles that will bring the story to life.

"The big room is a democracy," Brooks says. "You know an idea works when everyone agrees that it works. When everyone laughs, it's a good idea. It's a good sign. When no one laughs, that says something, too."

But there are both good and bad elements of the Group Think that takes place in writers' rooms. Downsides are that nuance can get completely lost, and subtlety overlooked, or that the "mission" of the room disappears. It's also hard to discuss intimate things that might ultimately lead to a great joke or a great line. And that is where the leader comes in, to help the room maintain its direction. "There has to be a leader because discipline is required to stay on track," Brooks emphasizes. And this is what *The Simpson*'s smaller room provides, namely discipline and story lines. He says the creation of a good story to work from aids the efforts of the writers in the big room tremendously.

Unlike other show runners, Brooks does not mind a quiet or somewhat negative person in his writers' room. He says, "Sometimes a negative force is someone who makes you try harder, someone you want to please or get a 'nod' from. Negative energy doesn't hurt the room—it can make people work that much more." And sometimes there are writers who don't know when to stop pitching the line or the joke they came up with. Brooks said that one of the smartest things he ever heard was on the set for *The Mary Tyler Moore Show* when a producer responded to a nagging writer by saying, "You know it works when everyone gets up and walks away, Bob." In other words, when the joke is right, it's right. And it will be obvious. But even so, some laughs—and they might even be big ones—may turn out to be just for the writers to enjoy, as they are too much of an "in" joke. These are designated as "room laughs" and the jokes that inspired them are likely never to be heard again.

Brooks believes there are dichotomies that emerge in the creative process. About his own individual process, he said, "Sometimes it's ecstasy and it's like someone is speaking through you." But there are other times, many other times, when he needs to just keep at it. "Even if you don't write for days, you have to respect that some things, some ideas, need to stew. And if you can't get anything going, maybe something is growing." But he says the best counsel he ever received about any kind of inability to write, writers block or whatever it's called, was from a "writer's writer" named Jerry Belson, who told him to just write, and no matter what else happened, to just keep writing. According to Brooks, the wisdom came in the form of these three words: "Lay Down S***."

To James L. Brooks, the job of creating, finally, is to get off your own back. He says, "The small miracle [of creativity] is that you sit down with nothing, and something comes. You come up with something. You have to embrace your fear, your fear of being bad—and roll over it." To him, and this was the pearl of the interview for me, he said, *"Real creativity is achieved not when you please others, but when you please yourself."*

His rooms have been among the most successful in the history of television, and the guidelines he uses to run them are a big part of the reason why.

Some James L. Brooks Rules of the Writers' Room

- The room is a democracy—it only likes what it likes
- Embrace fear—and roll over it
- Let a negative force inspire, and never intimidate
- Stay on track
- Trust your process and ". . . believe there are no mistakes"

Some James L. Brooks Tools of the Writers' Room

- Sometimes, two rooms. One high level, the other dialogue.
- A good leader, who is unafraid of/to discipline
- A mission, a focus, a clear path and purpose
- Constant search for story

As we neared the end of the conversation, I asked him what he would offer as guidance or wisdom to new creators, those just at the beginning of the journey. Or to those who might be stuck in a pattern and trying to change the way they think. Without a second's hesitation, he responded, "I would quote Samuel Beckett."

And here is the poem he would offer them . . .

No matter. Try again.
Fail again. Fail better.

ALLAN BURNS

Allan Burns is a very creative man. He started in Hollywood working for Jay Ward on *The Rocky and Bullwinkle Show*; then wrote for Leonard Stern on *Get Smart*; created *The Munsters*; won an Emmy for a completely forgotten show, *He and She*; and then changed the world of television by developing a new series for Grant Tinker's wife. Tinker was a producer on the Fox lot who was married to America's then-sweetheart, Mary Tyler Moore. He challenged several writers around Hollywood to come up with a three-camera show pilot and pitch it to her. As mentioned earlier, with James L. Brooks as his collaborator, Burns created *The Mary Tyler Moore Show*, one of the most successful shows in the history of television, which, over its eight-year run, earned four Emmys and led to three successful spin-offs (*Rhoda*, *Phyllis*, and *Lou Grant*). Funny, heartfelt, original, heartbreaking, and noted especially for its spectacular writing, the show was a hallmark of group creativity and collaboration, all of which grew from Allan Burns's well-run and very successful writers' room.

Over the years, Burns has participated in hundreds of writers' rooms. When I asked him what the key to a successful room was, and thus the key to successful group creativity, he shook his head, laughed, and said, "It's very simple. You can't be afraid to say anything. You cannot deny yourself the pleasure of a really good idea just because you are afraid to put it out there." How wise is that?

Of course, not every idea is going to be the greatest idea ever, but suppose you are able to gain the habit of confidence in your ideas. Suppose you never

233

judge yourself and your ability and creativity. Suppose you get out of your own way and allow your own thoughts and ideas to emerge freely from the rock of your intellect. It's not only possible, but also vital to participating in any room where you are expected to create and collaborate.

Allan Burns's Rules of the Writers' Room

- You can't be afraid to say *anything* or be nervous that your idea is stupid
- The room has to permit everyone to take a huge swing, and miss
- There will be some jewels, and some crap, as in everything
- The word that must not be heard in a writers' room is "no"
- *Listen* to the other people in the room. They might have a good idea or inspire a good idea— either way, you'll have to listen to hear it.

Allan Burns's Tools of the Writers' Room

- A big stack of index cards and a corkboard
- A car to drive around in and think of things

Burns described his tools simply. First is a big stack of blank index cards and the large corkboard on which to pin them. Each card gets an idea written on it and then up on the board it goes. This was the best way he knew how to develop a scene or a character, work out a joke or a story arc issue, or solve any dramatic problem. Whatever was needed ended up on a card, which ended up on the corkboard. He described the cards and corkboard as a net for all the ideas the room created. Soon enough, no matter what the dilemma, the board was full of cards. "You can easily arrange the ideas in varying sequences—until you start to see a show take place," he said. One of the most important things to see is "how the story emerges."

As for his second tool, his car, it is there behind the wheel that he would work out script problems while he was driving. This method is not recommended for all people, however. He said, "Somehow it always works. Sometimes it works really well, and sometimes you get in accidents."

Allan Burns's List of Things That Can Destroy a Writers' Room

- There are too many people
- The room lacks focus and purpose
- No one is clearly in charge
- There is too much interrupting

- The room is following several paths
- When the room goes on too long, soon it will be a room full of tired writers trying to do something better than what they did before they were tired

KEN LEVINE

At twenty-six, Ken Levine was named head writer of *M*A*S*H*. He went on to write and produce for an amazing list of shows including *Cheers*, *Frasier*, *Everybody Loves Raymond*, *Wings*, and, his heartbreaker, the ill-fated *Almost Perfect*. He is a straight shooter and tells it like it is. He has run writers' rooms for the past thirty years. As he described putting them together and how to run them, he sounded like an automobile mechanic describing a Rolls-Royce engine, someone who knew where everything was supposed to go and how each piece fit with every other one.

Levine routinely throws around terms like "stabbing the frog" or "Hey May." These are commonplace in the writers' world, especially among television writers, but largely unknown outside it. "Stabbing the Frog" means to write a joke to death. And "Hey May" is an homage to Carl Reiner, who wanted his viewers out in TV land to shout to their wives to come in from the kitchen and see what was on the television. Levine teaches a class for writers that instructs neophytes how to survive in the writers' room should they be lucky enough to ever get into one. It's a boot camp for creativity, including deadlines, meddling producers, and Chinese food at midnight. His depth of knowledge on how to facilitate and enable the best in creative comedic writing is extraordinary.

To fill a writers' room, Levine looks for people he would not mind being trapped in a Volkswagen bug with on a road trip across the country. He looks for funny people who work well with others. To keep the room spinning a little off balance, he wants a combination of people with huge egos and massive insecurities willing to work under tremendous pressure.

Levine looks to create "an atmosphere where no one is afraid. . . . People should not feel that every joke has to be the greatest one in the world. Even half a good idea could inspire someone else's even better idea."

Creative people bring with them their eccentricities, and this is their gift to the room. The role that Levine plays, whether as producer or show runner or head writer, is to first manage and protect *all* of the contributors who are in the room. He does this by trying to create an atmosphere where everyone feels they are free to speak and allowed to fail. The room must be wide open, physically and intellectually, in which all thoughts are allowed to emerge. Not everyone in the room will be perfectly organized and thinking in straight lines. People in the room might bounce around from subject to subject, topic to topic, and joke to joke. But for this to work, all ideas must be allowed to be presented as whole ideas without interruptions.

Ken Levine's Rules (of Etiquette) for a Writers' Room

- Pitch an idea only once, and move on
- Never censor yourself or one of your ideas. Pitch every idea that might work.
- Say it! Even a bad idea might lead to something.
- Avoid being the grammar police. It's a joy killer.
- The room is a team effort; it is not a competition
- Everyone in the room has to have thick skin
- Someone must "run" the room, or else—chaos
- Take regular breaks. Walk around, breathe, and refresh.
- No interrupting. Every idea should be presented as a whole idea.

Ken Levine's Must-Have Tools to Run a Writers' Room

- A secretary. He prefers to dictate his ideas, rather than pound them out at a keyboard. This lets them emerge and escape without having to go through his hands first.
- A shower. He said, "I solve more problems in the shower than anywhere else. I let my subconscious mind deal with the issues and I trust that it will figure them out."

SCOTT WINANT

Scott Winant is a respected film and television director and producer, most well known for his creation and Emmy Award–winning work on the show *thirtysomething*, in addition to *Huff* and *My So-Called Life*, as well as directing the first episode of *True Blood*. To him, the first responsibility of any filmmaker—and the director in particular—is to ensure that the collaborative efforts of all of the other people involved are working perfectly together to create a greater whole. If the director can get everyone on the team emotionally and intellectually invested, the project will only benefit. The director's responsibility is thus to build an environment in which all of the participants can freely and passionately create. Directing is the building of a very complex structure. Take out one piece and the whole thing might fall down. The director must show the rest of the cast and crew what thoughts are in his head, what ideas are there, what stories he wants to tell.

Scott Winant knows well how to turn weakness into strength. He had a learning disability as a child that kept him from reading until he was in the third grade. So up until then, all of his book reports were based on imaginary books by imaginary authors that he would then review and discuss at length. Because he was unable to read for himself, he became very visual; this process enabled a strong visual logic to guide his work. He had to become creative in order to be successful, both in his childhood and in his career.

According to him, "Creativity is . . . sharing through a specific medium what is inside your head. For instance, a painter sees a sunset. He interprets it (creates it) through his medium, the canvas and the paints, and people pay to see what he sees. Creativity is seeing things that have not been seen before, whether in your head or anywhere else. Successful creativity requires singularity of vision and then doing the work required to bring it into the world."

The mood and the success of any show is based on the mood and success of the writers' room. The show runner, who might also be the executive producer, is the one responsible for everything that happens in the writers' room. The best writers' rooms allow everyone to contribute—and they feel inclusive, not autocratic. Each writers' room has its own ecosystem. Some, like the writers' room for *30 Rock*, are encouraging and enabling. According to Winant, Tina Fey would not have someone in the room who was poison, even if he or she was very talented. She insists that her room be humane and kind. If a particular show is dry and biting, the writers' room can be just as cruel, if not more so, whereas other rooms, like the one he was in for *Frasier*, can be backstabbing, cutthroat, and competitive. He said the *Frasier* writers' room was intended to keep everyone uptight, just like the star was, and that Stephen Colbert's writers' room, on the other hand, maintains a simple and lasting guideline: "It's got to be all about F-U-N!!!"

At the conclusion of our meeting, Winant made this statement: "The process of making a film or television show is based on the creator's ability to *not fear inspiration*. But you can't just sit back and wait for it, either."

Scott Winant's Rules of the Writers' Room

- If you are secure in your own creativity, you won't be afraid of others' ideas
- Do not be afraid to tell whatever story is in your head. Use as many metaphors and analogies as you can think of to get people to see what's in there.
- The hardest thing about creativity is to accept that something is finished
- Constant rewrites only enable the law of diminishing returns
- In filmmaking, as in life, there are deadlines. Out of respect to the people who are signing the checks, you must meet the deadlines and finish on time.
- Do not fear inspiration

Scott Winant's Tools of the Writers' Room

- In a repeat of Allan Burns, Winant chose the storyboard—a miniature of the show told on index cards—as one of his most important tools. According to him, the storyboard reflects the thinking of both the director and the producer, and it encourages the writers to "see" the story that is in their heads as well.

- Group creativity is very much like group therapy. If the writers in the room feel that you are not being honest with your thoughts and ideas, they will *and should* turn on you.

THE ULTIMATE SET OF RULES FOR SUCCESSFUL COLLABORATIVE GROUP CREATIVITY

Because they are such amazing demonstrations of group creativity, comedic television writers' rooms are excellent templates for any act of group creativity or collaboration. As you have just read, they are filled with unique individuals, each with a strong and valued opinion. The rooms are open to any idea that is worth telling. The rooms respect honest opinions and love to see ideas improved and further built upon. Pure creativity has real value and garners the greatest respect. Deceit is like poison. Rooms have to be directed, and pointed in the right direction, because they cannot drive themselves. Overarching all of these ideas, however, is the fact that the room and all the individuals in it should have no fears. TV writers' rooms are not the only places where the rules of successful group creativity apply.

There are many challenging rooms that might limit creativity when actually they should only be trying to facilitate it. Advertising agencies with deadlines, and clients waiting for the details of new campaigns. Architecture firms filled with young dreamers who would like to change the world one building at a time. Lawyers' offices in the middle of important trials. Marketing companies fighting for a toehold against bigger, stronger rivals in an ever-shrinking revenue climate. Any business that is under threat from a disruptive technology and must reinvent itself and the way it does business in order to survive. All of these would benefit tremendously from better group thinking, more creativity, tangible collaborative successes, and inspiring environments that are able to recognize innovation.

All of the writer-producers I interviewed told me the same thing: fear has to be defeated if creativity is ever to thrive. Defeating fear is central to what *has* to happen if you are to take the wisdom of the writers' room and bring it successfully into whatever collaboration or group creativity you and your teammates are pursuing now or are about begin. Creativity is impossible if one is caught up in any doubt as to the value of the idea. Fear of any kind, of failure, of ridicule, of resentment, of embarrassment, of the unknown, or of anything else that freezes people and prevents their creativity, must be defeated.

But how? How can you create an environment that fosters creativity and distances itself from any kind of doubt or fear? The second-most-resounding guideline that each producer described does just that. Each said that a must-have to create a successful writers' room is an assurance that complete respect will be shown to all of the participants and all of the ideas that are presented. "Creativity is fragile, and the room is no different than a relationship—it has to have a flow, an honest exchange, based on mutual respect," said John Markus. So, forbidden are faint praise, dismissive compliments, use of the word "no," or any other responses that diminish either the idea or its creator. Just as important to him? Kindness. Kindness to yourself and others is a key to the room's success. "The factor of difficulty is so high, the standard of competition is so fierce," Markus continued, "that for the room to climb the mountain every week, as it needs to with a successful show, the tone in the room needs to reinforce that the writers revere each other's ideas."

Writers' rooms exist to foster creativity, to enable

it, to free it, to give it sanctuary. The rooms are incubators for new ideas. Everyone in the room can say, "What if we do this instead?" as many times as they like and still feel encouraged to say it again if that is what they feel they need to do. Every idea must begin its life treasured, at least in its early stages. Everyone needs to be listened to and heard. People need to be able to present the complete picture of what they are thinking. It goes without saying that most of the producers identified *listening to the whole idea* as the other most important thing the room can do to help itself.

The reason for this is because the last moments of someone's presentation of an idea are often a summarization of that same presentation. Sometimes this is actually a better telling of the story or idea than anything that preceded it. Somehow the summary forces the creator's idea to be shorter and sweeter, and in so doing, only the best elements rise to the top— yes—like cream.

So regardless of what your room looks like, or who is in it, or what stories you hope will emerge from it, there are seven simple guidelines you can follow that will allow your room to become more like a successful comedic television writers' room. They are:

- Be fearless with your own ideas
- Show complete respect for all others' ideas
- Be kind to everyone
- Let the room be a democracy
- Embrace every inspiration
- Stay on track
- Listen, and listen even more

If you can achieve these simple goals, the creativity that results will have a chance at greatness. This is true regardless of who you are or what sort of creativity you are after. Whether you are part of a group of advertising executives creating a campaign to sell more Cheerios, or a small army of architects designing a city center, or a team of writers and producers hoping to come up with a Broadway smash, your "writers' room" is the key to your success.

As we know from Mark Tramo, in a burst of creativity, the intellect is like an idea machine. Neurons fire and synapses connect. Glutamate, or one of the other excitatory substances, sprays everywhere and allows millions or billions of neural connections to take place. Out will tumble many possibilities, some good and some not so good, some on topic, some completely off. Thinking is the same process, regardless of the subject being thought about. Some other part of the brain determines quality or lasting value, and serves as the filter, deciding what is good, or not, or if what you think could sell, or not, and so on. But your brain itself, the machine of it, is functioning as designed the moment you begin to think thoughts you have never thought before, the moment your creativity rumbles to life.

The trick to successful group creativity, according to the experts with whom I consulted, is to get the intellects of several people up and running—all at the same time. This is one of the only ways that ideas can inspire other ideas and that thoughts never thought before become ideas illuminated like never before. The harmonics of thought, the great exchange of little ideas, the complete respect shown to others' ruminations, the fearlessness that replaces doubt: all of these become stepping-stones on the road to great group creativity.

A hit comedy television show is a miracle of timing and laughter, beauty and personality, and creativity nurtured into life, week after week, climbing the mountain again and again. The room that supports the hit show is no accident. It is a product of design and genius, humor and vulnerability, experts and luck, and matching several distinct personalities that "you wouldn't mind being stuck in a car with on a long road trip."

The triumph that is represented by a successful writers' room is extraordinary, and not surprisingly makes almost everyone involved a lot of money. Each of the writer/producers interviewed for this chapter is a multimillionaire, some several times over—not that money is everything, but it is not such a bad way to judge the value of their guidance. Their ideas have helped writers' rooms succeed over and over again. Fortunately, these ideas are simple and flexible enough to be used in any circumstance that requires a trusting and inspired collaboration, and serve as the ultimate example of collaborative group creativity.

CODA

WE HAVE JUST NOW, THIS SECOND, reached the limits of my knowledge on the subject of creativity. I hope to learn a great deal more, but at the moment, this is it. At least insofar as those things that I can share comfortably without ruining some friendships and exposing some very lucky and less talented writers. More than a few famous people I interviewed had absolutely no idea what happened when they were lost in their creative pursuits, and for this reason their big names were not dropped here.

I have nonetheless tried to cover the subject from every angle that I know of, not only as an individual pursuit but also how it exists and can succeed as a team sport in a group creativity situation. There are more differences between the two than I realized at the beginning of this writing, and more similarities than I could have possibly known, here at the end.

I hope you have enjoyed reading this book as much as I have enjoyed writing it. I also hope that your own creative passion is adorned with fresh options and interesting possibilities, more so than it has ever been before. With any luck, this will result in your next project being a great success, both personally and creatively.

TS

Los Angeles, 2014

ACKNOWLEDGMENTS AND THANK-YOUS

For reading the book in manuscript form, the kindest thing someone could ever do, and for offering meaningful insight and direction, I would like to thank these wonderful people:

Peter Zizzo
Linda Newmark
Preston Sturges
Susan Raihofer

Curtis Kin

Karen Sturges

Nicole Tibbetts

Mark Tramo

Gaby Moss

Professor D. Kern Holoman

Dr. Randall Sword

Chris Wright CBE

For providing me the circumstances in which to create and test out my ideas on creativity with their students, I would like to thank these teachers and administrators:

Patricia Ware

Anita Robertson

Rhonda Steinberg

Allison McDonald

Regina Boutte

Howard Lappin

Jennifer Parker

Carrie Fairbrother

Suzanne Claytor

Lannie Foster

Marguerite LaMotte

Vince Womack

For allowing me to interview and in some cases re-interview them on the subject of creativity and its infinite possibilities, and for sharing their knowledge on the subject, I would like to thank:

Alan and Marilyn Bergman
Kenny Edmonds
Allan Burns
Dennis Morgan
Ken Levine
Jay Sandrich
Sir George Martin
Tom Hattan
Alan Greenspan
Diane Warren
Paul Blake
Allee Willis
Dr. Mark Tramo
Kern Holoman
John Markus
Patricia Stroh
James L. Brooks
Scott Winant

For having the faith in me to complete the rough ideas I presented to you and your team, and for signing this book and ensuring its publication, I would like to thank Sara Carder and her very capable team at Tarcher/Penguin.

Last, but certainly not least, my thanks go out to the thousand-plus public school students I have had the privilege of working with, who allowed me to teach them creativity and push them to the edge of their comfort zone to achieve it. I mentored eighty-nine students out of this group throughout their high school years and they performed the songs we wrote again and again, at more than sixty events, including three for the president of the United States. Every one of these amazing young adults graduated from high school and was accepted to a four-year college, and eighty-four have since graduated. I am very proud of all of you, and thank you for your dedication.

KNOWLEDGE CONTAINED HEREIN COMES FROM ALL THESE PEOPLE

Alan and Marilyn Bergman

Alan Greenspan

Alan Livingston

Albert Einstein

Allan Burns

Allee Willis

Antoine de Saint-Exupéry

Antonina Armato

Beethoven

Bernie Taupin

Carole King

Clive Davis

Dennis Morgan

Diane Warren

Dr. Dre

Dr. Torsten Wiesel

Gerry Goffin

Gustave Eiffel

Irving Berlin

Itzhak Perlman

James L. Brooks

Jeff "Skunk" Baxter

John Marcus

Ken Levine

Kenneth "Babyface" Edmonds

Kim Peek

Larry Gelbart

Lamont Dozier

Leonard Bernstein

Mark Batson

Mark Tramo

Mark Twain

Michelangelo

Mozart

Neil Young

Paul Simon

Pablo Picasso

Rembrandt
Scott Winant
Simon Climie
Sir Elton John
Sir George Martin
Sir Paul McCartney
Stephen Sondheim
Wynton Marsalis

INDEX

ABOUT THE AUTHOR

TOM STURGES lives in Manhattan Beach, California, with his wife, Karen, and son, Kian.